LAW OF THE LAND

A Practical Legal Guide for Tourists and Business Travelers

Jamaica

By Michael L. Moore Esq.

Edited by Mindy Scarlett and Ally Knez-Siddique

Cover Design: Kristina Conatser

Published by: Law of the Land Publishing LLC

ISBN: 978-1-964870-01-4

DEDICATION

This book is dedicated to the memory of my late older brother, Kenneth Lee Moore, whose tragic murder at 15 years of age, inspired me to write these series of books.

This book is also dedicated to my parents, John Henry Moore, and Edna Mae Moore, whose tremendous parenting skills kept me focused on the important things in life, ... being reverent, getting educated, and prioritizing family.

Finally, this book is dedicated to my Beautiful family, my wife Royellen, my son AJ, and my daughter Karla. They inspire me every single day to be kind, patient, and compassionate.

IN LOVING MEMORY OF:

Belinda Joyce Moore Moss—My Beautiful and Wonderful Sister who supported me in every positive thing that I ever attempted to do.

Michael Eugene Baker—My Dedicated and Loyal Friend and Brother who always wanted the very Best for me.

Sylvia Joyce Hill—my eldest sister, who had a beautiful spirit and was like a second mother to me.

LAW OF THE LAND®

PUBLISHING for Tourists & Business Travelers

Travel smart. Stay legal. Stay safe.®

**From local laws to medical guides
we've got you covered world wide
in one digital platform.**

Travel Safe Anywhere
3 MONTHS FREE TRIAL

SCAN QR code
for more info

PREFACE

My introduction to the justice system came when I was only 10 years old. My 15-year-old brother was murdered with a butcher knife by a 19-year-old in a simple argument over a torn shirt. I was devastated by his death and sought retribution for his fate that never came. The woman was initially charged with second degree murder, but after plea negotiations, she was convicted of manslaughter and sentenced to only five years in a youthful offender school and ordered to undergo psychiatric care. That was it. Nothing more. The judicial system had run its course.

My family knew nothing about the justice system, and we did not have the tools to advocate for ourselves. No one provided us with a written source to reference for guidance through this process. There was no easily accessible, easy to understand, definitive source to use to educate ourselves about the legal system that we suddenly and unexpectedly found ourselves immersed in after being victimized by such a violent criminal act.

As I got older, finished college, law school, and ultimately started practicing law, it became clear to me that most people are not knowledgeable about the law or how the judicial process works. If most people are uninformed here in the United States regarding the law and the legal process, how would they fare when in other countries? I realized that tourists and businesspeople who travel internationally needed access to information on how to navigate the legal system in other countries!

For many years, there has been considerable media attention focused on international travelers experiencing legal difficulties while traveling abroad. Most of these news stories gained attention in the United States and abroad because they involved American citizens facing punishment that was considered "unconventional" and "harsh" by United States' legal standards. I recall a news story in 1994 regarding Michael Fay, a young American male, who had broken the law in Singapore. He was convicted and sentenced to be caned and or whipped publicly. While the United States Government weighed in on the inappropriate and cruel nature of the punishment, the young American was beaten because he had been convicted under Singapore law.

Similarly, in recent years, international news stories have garnered headlines regarding foreign travelers and their issues with the laws of countries that were not their own. Amanda Knox, an American woman, was accused of murdering her roommate in Italy in 2007 and spent almost four years in an Italian prison before being definitively acquitted by the Supreme Court of Cassatio. Kenneth Bae, an American citizen, was arrested in North Korea in 2012 and was convicted for hostile acts against the communist country. He was sentenced to 15 years hard labor but was released in 2014 after efforts by the U.S. State Department. More recently, United States Basketball Star, Brittany Griner was arrested in February 2022 at a Moscow airport on drug-related charges and detained for nearly 10 months, spending much of that time in prison. Her plight unfolded at the same time Russia invaded Ukraine and further heightened tensions between Russia and the United States, ending only after she was freed in exchange for a notorious Russian arms dealer.

It was in 1994 that another personal tragic event occurred that also inspired me to write these series of books. A dear friend and client of mine was brutally murdered while on his second honeymoon in Jamaica. News of his murder shocked me and our local community. The legal hurdles his family had to overcome to see that justice was properly dispensed far away from home, in another country, with an entirely different set of criminal procedural rules and laws, was difficult to navigate.

As I was my friend's attorney at the time of his death, his family asked that I act as their "legal liaison" to the Jamaican Prosecutor's Office and to the Jamaican Police Department. I participated in multiple police interviews with my client's widow because she was the primary witness to his murder. As a former prosecuting attorney, I was also allowed by the Court, as a professional courtesy, to sit at the prosecutor's table to consult with the prosecuting attorney during trial. What I observed about the Jamaican trial process from a front row seat was compelling enough to cause me to seriously consider educating the "world" regarding what to expect and how to act appropriately when faced with legal issues while traveling abroad.

One of the realities in life is that, regardless of what country you are in, it is never a pleasant experience to run afoul of the law and be forced to accept that someone else will be making a decision about your pecuniary, proprietary, or penal interests (your money, your property, or your freedom).

It is important to know what the laws are, how they apply to you, and how to navigate the legal system if you are charged with a crime. It is also very helpful to know what resources are available to you if you are the victim of a criminal act. At the end of the day, an "ounce of prevention is worth a pound of cure," so the more knowledge you have, the more ammunition you possess, and the more likely you will have a positive outcome.

If you are traveling to Jamaica, the first thing you should pack is a copy of this book! The helpful information and tips contained in this volume will provide a great starting point for knowing what to do (and not to do!) when you arrive at your destination and will help ensure that you have a wonderful vacation or business trip unmarred by tangles with the law.

TABLE OF CONTENTS

INTRODUCTION

INTRODUCTION

As a practicing attorney for over 34 years, I have represented numerous clients who travel often but are unaware of the laws of the land they are traveling to.

Therefore, many years ago, I decided to write a series of books that would explain the laws of specific countries. My focus was to explain the laws that may affect travelers in a straightforward manner, without all of the legal language that is sometimes hard for even seasoned attorneys to understand.

About This Book

The aim of this book is simple: it provides you, the traveler, with a simple, easy to read book that will provide a basic legal guide that explains the law in the country that you are about to visit. It is not intended to educate you on ALL of the laws in a given country, the goal is to provide you with the details of the most common legal and safety issues faced by tourists and business travelers.

I have also provided context with background information on places not to visit, statistics on the country as well as prevention measures you should take to safeguard your legal and physical safety. Knowledge is a powerful thing and knowing how to stay out of trouble (or how to get out of it!) is important for everyone who travels.

This *Law of The Land/Jamaica* book simply helps you become more informed about your legal rights, responsibilities, and obligations in a wide range of subject areas.

Last, but not least, this book does NOT purport to offer legal advice. It does, however, provide the information you need to stay safe, follow the law and how to navigate around legal difficulties. However, if you do face legal difficulties, the information in this book will provide you with a starting point for solving the problem and obtaining legal assistance should it be required.

Hypotheticals Used Throughout This Book

From time to time throughout this book, I will explain the law to readers by using hypothetical scenarios. These hypotheticals will be marked by an icon that will be explained in further detail as you read on.

How This Book is Organized

CHAPTER 1: **About Jamaica.** This chapter will provide you with a brief overview about Jamaica and its history. It also addresses the best way to travel to Jamaica, Visa requirements, monetary advice, and the best times to visit.

CHAPTER 2: **Customs.** This chapter will provide information on what to expect when entering Jamaica and documentation that is required. It will also explain what restricted and prohibited items are when entering Jamaica along with what must be declared when returning to your destination from Jamaica.

CHAPTER 3: **Crime in Jamaica.** This chapter provides an overview of the history of crime in Jamaica and steps that Jamaican officials have taken to curb the high rate of crime.

CHAPTER 4: **Criminal Law Violations.** This chapter will provide information on drug offenses, primarily marijuana and cannabis products, penalties, and questions and answers about marijuana.

CHAPTER 5: **Alcohol-Related Offenses.** This chapter will provide key points regarding the sale, consumption, and regulations of alcohol use in Jamaica.

CHAPTER 6: **Firearm & Ammunition Offenses.** This chapter will provide key points regarding the possession of firearms and ammunition in Jamaica.

CHAPTER 7: **Prostitution.** This chapter provides an overview of the history of prostitution in Jamaica, laws and penalties, prostitution practices, sex trafficking, sex tourism, and health in Jamaica, tips to avoid being hassled, a Law of the Land Hypothetical, and the current situation on prostitution in Jamaica.

CHAPTER 8: **LGBTQ.** This chapter will provide information regarding the acceptance of LGBTQ people in Jamaica, and the laws surrounding homosexuality.

CHAPTER 9: **Sexually Motivated/Violent Crimes.** This chapter will provide an overview of sexually related crimes in Jamaica.

CHAPTER 10: **Arrested in Jamaica.** This chapter will provide information on what to do if you are arrested in Jamaica.

CHAPTER 11: **Jails vs. Prisons: Conditions & Culture.** This chapter will provide information on the conditions and culture of Jamaican Jails and Prisons.

CHAPTER 12: **Helping a Friend or Relative Imprisoned in Jamaica.** This chapter will provide information on how you can assist a friend or relative imprisoned in Jamaica.

CHAPTER 13: **The Administration of Justice.** This chapter will provide information on Jamaica's Judicial System.

CHAPTER 14: **Crime Victim Assistance.** This chapter will provide information on crime victim assistance along with providing safety tips.

CHAPTER 15: **Police.** This chapter will provide information on the Jamaican Police and how to report a crime.

CHAPTER 16: **How to Get Legal Help in Jamaica.** This chapter will provide information regarding how to obtain legal assistance for travelers to Jamaica.

CHAPTER 17: **Medical Facilities & Hospitals.** This chapter will provide information about how to obtain medical care while visiting Jamaica.

CHAPTER 18: **Driving in Jamaica.** This chapter will provide information on Driving in Jamaica, it's Traffic Rules, and Road Safety Tips.

CHAPTER 19: **Nude Beaches & Clothing-Optional Resorts.** This chapter will provide an overview of Nude beaches in Jamaica, and the legality and safety of visiting Nude beaches in Jamaica.

CHAPTER 20: **Unusual Laws.** This chapter will provide information on some Unusual Laws in Jamaica, and penalties and fines.

CHAPTER 21: **Traveling Safely.** This chapter will provide information on women traveling alone, crime prevention for families, safety notes for all travelers, and overall advice.

CHAPTER 22: **Tourist Taxation.** This chapter will provide information on taxes that tourists are required to pay in Jamaica.

CHAPTER 23: **Long-Term Stays.** This chapter will provide an overview of the consequences for overstaying your visit to Jamaica.

CHAPTER 24: **Civil Litigation.** This chapter will provide information about the civil litigation process in Jamaica.

CHAPTER 25: **Other Things to Know.** This chapter will provide information on the harassment of tourists, travel and safety, and other practical tips.

CHAPTER 26: **Quick Reference Guide.** This chapter is a quick way to get information. It is a condensed version of the chapters in this book.

Emergency/Important Contact Numbers in Jamaica

Useful Jamaican Patois Phrases

Glossary

Icons Used in this Book

What do those pictures throughout the book mean? See below:

WARNING: This icon flags information about things you should avoid while visiting Jamaica. Heed the advice next to this icon to avoid legal perils.

REMEMBER: This icon flags noteworthy information that you shouldn't forget.

HELPFUL TIPS: This icon flags information that will help you when entering Jamaica, relates to a legal situation, or refers to resources available while visiting Jamaica.

TECHNICAL INFORMATION: This icon flags technical aspects of the law. If you are faced with a legal problem, and you want to learn more about the law involved, this information can be helpful.

 **ADDITIONAL INFORMATION**: This icon points to the location of additional information available on the internet.

 **HYPOTHETICAL**: This icon points to hypothetical scenarios to illustrate possible legal problems and the outcome.

 **QUESTIONS**: This icon points to questions and answers throughout the book.

 **TRUE STORY**: This icon points to true events throughout the book.

Where to Go From Here

If you have a specific question about the law in Jamaica as it relates to a specific area, just turn to the chapter that addresses that issue or turn to the Quick Reference Guide.

You can also read the book from cover to cover to obtain a more comprehensive understanding of the Jamaican laws and resources available should you find yourself in a legal predicament while visiting.

 **Disclaimer:** While the recommendations in this book primarily address U.S. citizens, the information is relevant and applicable to citizens of any country.

ABOUT JAMAICA

- About Jamaica
- Jamaica, the Basics
- Jamaica's Hospitality

ABOUT JAMAICA

About Jamaica

Jamaica, a Caribbean Island nation, has a lush topography of mountains, rainforests and reef-lined beaches. Many of its all-inclusive resorts are clustered in Montego Bay, with its British-colonial architecture, and Negril, known for its diving and snorkeling sites. Jamaica is famed as the birthplace of reggae music, and its capital Kingston is home to the Bob Marley Museum, dedicated to the famous singer.

Jamaica is the third largest of the Caribbean islands, and the largest English-speaking Island in the Caribbean Sea. It is situated 90 miles south of Cuba, 600 miles south of Florida, and 100 miles southwest of Haiti. Jamaica is approximately 146 miles long, 51 miles wide, and has an area of 4,411 square miles. The capital, Kingston, is the largest city and is in the southeastern part of the island.

The island's name comes from the Arawak word Xaymaca, which means "land of wood and water" or "land of springs." Jamaica, an island in the Caribbean, was originally inhabited by the Arawak and Taino peoples before Christopher Columbus arrived in 1494. It became a Spanish colony but was taken over by the British in 1655. Jamaica thrived on sugar plantations worked by enslaved Africans, who greatly influenced the island's culture. Jamaica gained independence from the United Kingdom in 1962 and has since become known for its vibrant culture, reggae music, and strong national identity.

Jamaica's multi-racial population of almost 2.5 million is mostly made of African, European, East Indian, and Chinese cultures. Hence, the country's motto is "Out of Many, One People." In Jamaica, the official language is English, but most people speak Jamaican Patois (also called Jamaican Creole) in everyday conversation. Patois is a blend of English, African languages, and other influences, and is known for its unique pronunciation and grammar.

Religion in Jamaica is predominantly Christian, with most Jamaicans identifying as Protestant along with a significant Roman Catholic population. The Rastafari movement, which originated in Jamaica in the 1930s, also plays a major cultural and spiritual role. Rastafari combines African heritage, Christianity, and Afrocentric beliefs, focusing on the divinity of Emperor Haile Selassie I of Ethiopia. It promotes unity, resistance to oppression, and a return to Africa, often expressed through reggae music, dreadlocks, and the use of marijuana. Additionally, there are smaller communities of Muslims, Hindus, and those practicing indigenous spiritual beliefs.

Jamaica offers a mixed affordability landscape for both residents and visitors. On average, the cost of living in Jamaica is approximately 33.2% lower than in the United States, making it relatively affordable for expatriates and locals alike.[1] Monthly expenses for a single person, excluding rent, amount to around J$291,245, reflecting a comfortable yet budget-conscious lifestyle.[2] Housing costs vary significantly; for instance, renting a one-bedroom apartment in the city center ranges from J$35,000 to J$200,000 per month, while options outside the center can start as low as J$25,000.[3] Food and transportation are generally more economical compared to many Western countries, with a basic meal at an inexpensive restaurant costing approximately J$500 to J$2,250. For tourists, day-to-day expenses, including meals, entertainment, and transportation, can be manageable, although prices in tourist-centric areas may be higher.

---

1   https://www.mylifeelsewhere.com/cost-of-living/united-states/jamaica

2   https://www.expatistan.com/cost-of-living/country/jamaica

3   https://jamaica-homes.com/docs/what-is-the-cost-of-living-in-jamaica/

Jamaica, Irresistible Travel Destination

Jamaica, a jewel in the Caribbean, weaves a tapestry of experiences that cater to the diverse tastes of every traveler. From the magnetic charm of its beaches to the rhythmic beats of reggae, the island stands as a beacon for those seeking an unforgettable escape. In 2022, Jamaica welcomed approximately 3.3 million visitors, comprising 2 million stopover arrivals and 855,000 cruise passengers, whose combined spending contributed to the destination earning US$3.7 billion.

Many visitors to Jamaica have expressed appreciation for the warmth and friendliness of the local people. The hospitality and positive attitude of Jamaicans are often highlighted as a memorable aspect of the travel experience. Travelers also recount their experiences of immersing themselves in Jamaica's vibrant music scene, attending reggae concerts, and participating in music festivals. The reggae culture is deeply ingrained in the local lifestyle, and visitors find joy in embracing it.

Montego Bay is the most traveled-to city in Jamaica. It's a tourist hotspot with an overwhelming number of resorts and hotels. It is where cruise ships dock and most international flights land. The location is very convenient with it being in between Ocho Rios and Negril, making it a great place to stay and go on day trips.

Jamaica, The Basics

How to Get There

Jamaica has three international airports: Norman Manley International Airport in Kingston, Sangster International Airport in Montego Bay, and Ian Fleming International Airport close to Ocho Rios.

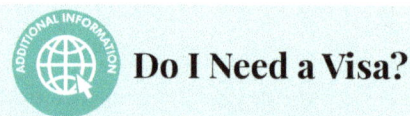

Do I Need a Visa?

According to the site **https://www.ivisa.com/jamaica**, if you have a United States Passport, you do NOT need a visa. All visitors are required to travel with a return or onward ticket for entry into Jamaica. For more information, go to: **http://www.congenjamaica-ny.org/visas/requirements-2/**. Other nationalities can visit this site to see what the protocol is for other countries.

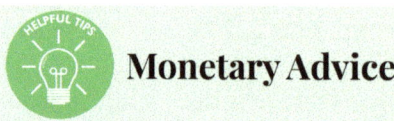

Monetary Advice

Be sure that you take cash, as some places do NOT accept credit cards. The currency in Jamaica is the Jamaican Dollar which currently changes for about J$110 to US$1, (be sure to get an update, as this may change). There are currency exchanges spread out all through the city so do not worry about exchanging money (bring in USD). However, it is a commonly known fact that using money exchanges in Jamaican cities offer a better experience (and less costs!) than using the money exchange at the airport. Last, but not least, bargaining is not only accepted, it is welcomed!

When to Visit?

The climate in Jamaica is hot, oppressive, windy, and partly cloudy. Over the course of the year, the temperature typically varies from 73°F to 89°F and is rarely below 71°F or above 91°F. Based on the beach/pool score, the best time of year to visit Jamaica for hot-weather activities is from mid-December to mid-April. The rainiest time is from August to November, as this is hurricane season. (If you don't mind getting wet, this is the best time to shop for resort deals!) It is Carnival in April, Bob Marley Birthday Week in February, and Reggae Sunfest in July, so pick the time that best fits your interests.

Jamaica's Hospitality

Jamaica is known for its warm hospitality, with locals often going out of their way to make visitors feel welcome. Whether you're staying in a luxury resort, a boutique hotel, or an eco-lodge, you'll find a range of accommodation options to suit different budgets and preferences. The island is also a popular stop for cruise ships, with ports in Ocho Rios, Montego Bay, and Falmouth, where passengers can explore local attractions during short visits.

Jamaicans express hospitality through warmth, generosity, and a welcoming attitude. It's common for locals to greet visitors with a friendly smile, a handshake, or even a hug, and they often take the time to ask how you're doing or show genuine interest in your well-being. Offering help is a natural part of Jamaican hospitality, whether it's guiding visitors to a location, offering food or drinks, or simply sharing local knowledge. Guests are often invited into homes where they may be treated to a home-cooked meal, with dishes like jerk chicken, rice and peas, and fresh fruit. In addition to verbal expressions, Jamaicans frequently use their language, often calling someone "mi fren" (my friend) to convey friendship and warmth. Hospitality in Jamaica is deeply rooted in a sense of community, where making others feel comfortable and appreciated is a priority.

Jamaica's combination of friendly people, diverse accommodations, and accessible tourist spots make it a popular destination for relaxation, adventure, and cultural experiences. Visitors are drawn to its beautiful landscapes, vibrant culture, and the chance to experience both tranquility and excitement.

CHAPTER 2

CUSTOMS

IN THIS CHAPTER

- Travelers Entering Jamaica
- Customs Entitlements and Monetary Restrictions
- Money and Monetary Instruments
- Restricted and Prohibited Items
- Five Practical Tips to Know Before You Go
- General Questions
- Law of the Land Hypothetical

CUSTOMS

Travelers Entering Jamaica

 All passengers arriving in Jamaica are required to present their passport, along with the completed Customs Declaration Form (C5) to a Customs Officer for processing. You should respond truthfully to all questions and accurately declare what is in their possession. This includes a requirement to report any food, plants, animal products, and monetary instruments (cash, cheques, money orders) of US$10,000, its equivalent or more.

To enter Jamaica as a tourist, you'll need a valid passport (with at least six months validity) and a return or onward ticket. Most tourists from countries like the U.S., Canada, the UK, and the EU don't need a visa for stays of up to 90 days. You may also need to show proof of sufficient funds and provide details of your accommodation.

Health requirements, such as a yellow fever vaccination, may apply if you're coming from certain countries. Upon arrival, you'll go through immigration, where an officer will check your documents and ask a few questions about your stay. After collecting your baggage, you'll proceed through customs and declare any items as needed.

With everything in order, you're ready to head out of the airport! Jamaica has plenty of transportation options at the airport, including taxis, shuttle buses, and rental cars. You can also arrange a transfer through your hotel or a tour operator in advance. Tip: make sure to check for any updated travel requirements before you go. Welcome to Jamaica!

Customs Entitlements and Monetary Restrictions

Each passenger aged 18 or older is eligible for duty concessions on the following items:

- A US$500 duty-free allowance for personal and household items that are not intended for resale or in commercial quantities.
- Instruments and tools required for their profession, trade, occupation, or employment, as long as these items have been in the passenger's possession and for genuine use for at least six (6) months.

Money and Monetary Instruments

Passengers are allowed to bring money and monetary instruments into or out of Jamaica but must adhere to certain regulations. If you are traveling with US$10,000 or more (or its equivalent), you are required to:

1. Declare the amount on your Immigration/Customs Declaration Form (I/C5) to the Jamaica Customs Agency.

2. Fill out the Financial Investigation Division Cross Border Form (provided by a Customs Officer).

3. Provide proof of the source of the funds.

4. Declare the intended use of the funds.

 Failure to comply with these regulations is considered a violation of the Jamaica Customs Act and may result in fines or penalties.

 ## Restricted and Prohibited Items

When entering Jamaica, certain items are prohibited, including illegal drugs, firearms, counterfeit goods, obscene materials, and products made from endangered species. Restricted items include alcohol, tobacco, large amounts of cash (over US$10,000), certain food products, prescription medications (which must be accompanied by a doctor's note), and plants or seeds. Always check the latest guidelines before traveling to ensure you comply with customs regulations!

 ## Five Practical Tips to Know Before You Go

1. While the Jamaican dollar (JMD) is the official currency, US dollars are widely accepted. It's still a good idea to have some local currency for small purchases. Credit and debit cards are also commonly used in most tourist areas.

2. Jamaica doesn't require specific vaccinations for entry, but it's a good idea to get routine vaccines like Hepatitis A and Typhoid. Also, drink bottled water to avoid stomach issues, especially if you're not used to the local tap water.

3. Jamaica is warm year-round, so pack light, breathable clothing, sunscreen, and a hat. If you're visiting during the rainy season (May to November), bring a rain jacket and waterproof shoes. Don't forget insect repellent, especially if you're staying near nature reserves or rural areas.

4. Jamaicans are known for their friendly hospitality, so greeting people with a smile and a "hello" goes a long way. It's also customary to tip hotel staff, drivers, and guides. A 10-15% tip is common for good service.

5. Stick to well-traveled tourist areas and avoid venturing into less-populated areas, especially at night. When using local transportation, it's safer to book official taxis or use hotel transfers. Make sure to agree on a fare before starting the journey.

 **General Questions**

1. *Should I pay custom dues for money and other monetary-equivalent instruments I bring into Jamaica?* It depends. If you are bringing more than US$10,000, or its equivalent, you must declare it and pay custom dues.

2. *Are there tax-free/duty-free stores in Jamaica that tourists can take advantage of while visiting in Jamaica?* Yes. These stores will be usually near a port of entry, such as an airport or close to shipping docks. Under the Duty-Free Shopping System Act, the Commissioner of Customs is empowered to license shops to sell duty-free items to tourists.

 **https://www.cbp.gov/travel/international-visitors/ kbyg/types-exemptions**

 **Law of the Land Hypothetical**

HYPOTHETICAL: *Say you received a US$700 bracelet as a gift, and you bought a US$40 hat and a US$60 color print. Because these items total US$800, you would not be charged duty, since you have not exceeded your duty-free exemption. If you had also bought a US$500 painting on that trip, you could bring all US$1,300 worth of merchandise home without having to pay duty, because fine art is duty-free.*

CRIME IN JAMAICA

- Overview
- Crime Hotspots in Jamaica
- Crime Statistics
- Quick Safety Tips

CHAPTER 3

CRIME IN JAMAICA

Overview

Jamaica, with its picturesque landscapes and vibrant culture, also grapples with some significant challenges related to crime. The country has garnered international attention for having one of the world's highest per-capita murder rates. In 2010, a state of emergency cast a harsh spotlight on the violent gang and drug culture in Kingston, the nation's capital. This scrutiny illuminated the complex web of factors contributing to violent crime, including gangs, drug trafficking, political unrest, poverty, and retaliatory actions.

The prevalence of violent crime extends beyond Kingston, affecting popular tourist destinations like Montego Bay, Negril, and Ocho Rios. While many crimes involve Jamaicans targeting fellow citizens and are linked to issues such as drugs, gangs, and politics, visitors are not entirely exempt from security concerns. Crimes against tourists in these tourist-centric areas tend to be property-oriented, such as pickpocketing and petty theft. However, armed robberies, though infrequent, have occurred, and resistance by victims may escalate these incidents into violent confrontations.

In response to the safety challenges faced by tourists, special tourist police have been deployed in popular areas. Easily identifiable by their distinctive uniform featuring white hats, white shirts, and black pants, these officers aim to maintain a visible presence to deter criminal activities.

Despite these efforts, it is crucial for travelers to remain vigilant and take precautions against potential risks.

While property crimes are more prevalent in tourist hotspots, it's essential to acknowledge that violent crime, including sexual assault, remains a broader issue across Jamaica. Cities like Kingston and Montego Bay face higher incidents of such crimes, exacerbated by the challenges of an understaffed and resource-limited police force. The presence of gated resorts does not provide complete immunity, emphasizing the need for travelers to exercise caution even within seemingly secure environments.

 In light of these safety concerns, visitors are urged to visit the United States Department of State's website, (or its equivalent in other countries), at **https://www.state.gov/**, for updates on the "safety status" for visiting Jamaica, prior to visiting, and prioritize their well-being by staying informed about local conditions, adhering to recommended safety guidelines, and remaining vigilant in various settings. This includes being aware of one's surroundings, practicing discretion with valuables, and avoiding risky areas, especially during nighttime. While the allure of Jamaica's natural beauty and cultural richness is undeniable, travelers should approach their visit with a balanced perspective that considers both the positive aspects and the need for cautious exploration.

Crime Hotspots in Jamaica

Overall, Jamaica is considered safe to visit, especially in well-established tourist areas. The country draws millions of visitors each year who enjoy its vibrant culture, beautiful beaches, and friendly locals.

However, like any destination, there are certain areas with higher crime rates, particularly outside tourist zones, where violence or theft can be more common. The most common safety concerns for tourists are petty theft, such as pickpocketing or bag snatching, especially in crowded areas. Violent crime can occur, but it is often concentrated in specific neighborhoods, many of which are far from the usual tourist routes.

Here are some of the major crime hotspots that visitors should be aware of:

1. **Kingston (certain areas)**: Kingston, the capital, has some areas with higher crime rates, particularly in neighborhoods like **Tivoli Gardens, Trench Town**, and **Riverton City**. These areas can experience gang violence and should be avoided by tourists, especially after dark.

2. **Montego Bay (certain parts)**: Montego Bay, a popular tourist destination, also has neighborhoods with higher crime rates, such as **Flankers, Norwood**, and **Rose Heights**. While the main tourist areas like **Mobay's Hip Strip** are generally safe, it's best to avoid venturing into these high-risk neighborhoods.

3. **Spanish Town:** Known for its history, Spanish Town also struggles with violent crime in certain parts, such as **Old Capital**. It's a town worth visiting for its cultural heritage but should be approached with caution, particularly if you're unfamiliar with the area.

4. **Portmore:** Portmore, a residential area near Kingston, has seen an increase in gang-related activity and violent crime in some parts. While parts of Portmore are safe for tourists, it's better to stay within well-known, tourist-friendly areas.

5. **Ocho Rios (some surrounding areas)**: Ocho Rios, another well-known tourist hotspot, is generally safe, but like all tourist destinations, there are some areas where crime can be an issue, particularly in **outlying areas** away from the main attractions. Stick to popular resorts and attractions like **Dunn's River Falls** and **Ocho Rios Bay Beach**.

Crime Statistics

Jamaica, like many countries, has faced ongoing challenges with crime, but the situation is complex and varies across different areas of the island. Over the years, violent crime, particularly **gang-related violence**, has been a major concern. **Homicides**, often linked to gang turf wars and organized crime, remain a significant issue, especially in cities like Kingston, Montego Bay, and Spanish Town. Despite efforts by the Jamaican government to curb violence, such as states of emergency and community policing initiatives, these areas continue to experience high levels of violent crime, contributing to Jamaica's elevated homicide rate in comparison to other countries in the Caribbean.

However, it's not just gang violence that poses a concern. **Robbery** and **theft** are widespread issues, particularly in tourist-heavy areas. Tourists are often at risk for petty crimes like **pickpocketing**, **muggings**, and **car thefts**, especially in crowded locations such as beaches, markets, and public transport hubs. While these crimes are typically non-violent, they can still disrupt a visitor's experience.

Sexual assault and **rape** are also concerns, but these crimes are more prevalent in local communities than in areas frequently visited by tourists. Still, it's advised for travelers to avoid wandering into unfamiliar or poorly lit areas, especially at night.

On top of violent crime and theft, scams have also been on the rise, with **fraudulent tour operators** or **fake accommodation** offers targeting unsuspecting tourists. As more people turn to online platforms for booking, these types of **cybercrimes** have become more common.

Crime statistics in Jamaica reveal a complex and concerning landscape of public safety, particularly with regards to violent crimes such as murder, robbery, and shootings. Recent studies have highlighted a significant trend in violent crime rates, as well as the use and prevalence of firearms in these offenses. The need for urgent action to address these issues is underscored by alarming statistics that indicate a persistent challenge in ensuring public safety.

The analysis of violent crimes from 2010 to 2022 shows that Jamaica has seen fluctuations in crime rates, with a peak in the murder rate occurring in 2017, registering 60.37 per 100,000 people. Since 2018, the nation has experienced an average of four murders per day, which translates to one murder every six hours, highlighting the dire state of public safety in the country.[4]

Guns have emerged as the predominant weapon of choice in many violent crimes, with 81.1% of violent incidents involving firearms. The prevalence of guns in robberies, murders, and shootings further illustrates the critical necessity for stronger gun control measures and initiatives aimed at reducing illegal firearms trafficking in Jamaica. This reliance on firearms in violent crimes not only exacerbates the danger faced by citizens but also complicates crime prevention efforts. However, despite the challenges, there has been a noted decline in violent crime occurrences between 2010 and 2022, showing a 43.7% reduction in daily murders, robberies, and shootings.

Many tourists still have positive and trouble-free experiences in Jamaica. The government and tourism authorities have taken significant steps to make popular tourist areas safer, with an increased police presence and better security measures around resorts and attractions. The hospitality and friendliness of the Jamaican people remain key reasons why the island continues to attract millions of visitors each year. However, it's always recommended to stay informed, follow local safety advice, and exercise caution, particularly in areas known for crime.

---

4   https://jcf.gov.jm/
    an-analysis-of-select-violent-crimes-in-jamaica-2010-2022

 ## Quick Safety Tips

- **Stay within well-known tourist areas:** Stick to popular resorts, beaches, and attractions, especially if you're unfamiliar with the area.

- **Travel with a guide or in groups:** If you're going to explore more remote areas, it's always better to go with a local guide or as part of a group tour.

- **Avoid walking alone at night:** It's safer to travel by taxi or arranged transport after dark.

- **Use reputable transportation:** Book taxis through your hotel or reputable companies to ensure safety.

CRIMINAL LAW VIOLATIONS

CHAPTER 4

CRIMINAL LAW VIOLATIONS

Marijuana and Other Drugs in Jamaica

Jamaica, renowned for its association with **marijuana** and colloquially referred to as a weed haven, has unique legal regulations surrounding cannabis. Despite its cultural significance, marijuana remains illegal in the country. However, there have been noteworthy adjustments to the legal landscape, offering a nuanced perspective on possession and use.

In 2015, the Jamaican government enacted changes to marijuana laws, reclassifying possession of small amounts—up to two ounces or 56.6 grams—as a petty offense, subject to a fine rather than criminal prosecution. Possession of larger quantities or other illicit drugs, however, the possession of more than 56 grams of ganja remains a criminal offence, and a person can be criminally charged and tried for it. If found guilty, they are liable to a prison sentence, a fine, or both, and will have it written in a criminal record. Notably, the law permits the cultivation of up to five marijuana plants for medical purposes, reflecting a progressive stance on medicinal cannabis.

People who visit Jamaica can use medical marijuana, but only after been granted a permit. This permit allows tourists to purchase and carry up to two ounces of cannabis at a given time, for personal and medical purposes only. Visitors must also show a document from a recognized medical practitioner that proves their use of medical cannabis for a specific condition. Tourists can also sign a voluntary declaration to acknowledge their use of medical cannabis, and this usually includes a fee.

 Delta-8 tetrahydrocannabinol, also known as delta-8 THC, is a psychoactive substance found in the Cannabis sativa plant, of which marijuana and hemp are two varieties. Delta-8 THC is one of over 100 cannabinoids produced naturally by the cannabis plant but is not found in significant amounts in the cannabis plant. As a result, concentrated amounts of delta-8 THC are typically manufactured from hemp-derived cannabidiol (CBD). Simply put, Delta 8 is a Cannabis product.

Delta-8 THC is not specifically mentioned in Jamaica's cannabis laws, which focus mainly on cannabis and its derivatives like CBD. As a relatively new product, Delta-8 falls into a legal grey area, with no clear guidelines on its status. Since Jamaica allows medical cannabis under certain regulations, travelers should be cautious when bringing Delta-8 products into the country, as they may be subject to scrutiny. It's safest to check with local authorities or avoid bringing such items.

In Jamaica, the laws surrounding **illegal drugs**, beyond marijuana, are strict and carry severe consequences. Possessing substances like cocaine, heroin, ecstasy, or methamphetamine is against the law and can lead to serious penalties, including imprisonment and heavy fines. Drug trafficking, which involves transporting or distributing illegal drugs, is considered a major offense, often resulting in lengthy prison sentences or life imprisonment, depending on the severity of the crime. The use of illicit drugs is also heavily penalized, with users at risk of arrest and prosecution. Jamaican authorities maintain a strong stance against drug-related crimes, with active enforcement to combat the illegal drug trade. For tourists, it's essential to avoid any involvement with illegal drugs, as the country's zero-tolerance policy ensures strict repercussions for such offenses.

Prescription Medication

If you're planning to bring prescription medication to Jamaica, it's generally allowed, but there are some important steps to ensure a smooth process. First, you should carry your original prescription along with the medication in its original packaging, clearly labeled with your name. This helps to avoid any confusion at customs. However, if your medication contains controlled substances—such as certain narcotics or sedatives—you'll need to have a doctor's note confirming that it's for personal use. In some cases, you may also need to seek authorization from Jamaica's Ministry of Health before bringing it into the country.

It's also important to note that you should only bring a reasonable quantity for personal use during your stay. Bringing in larger amounts could raise suspicion and lead to complications. Lastly, always declare your medication at customs, if necessary, as failing to do so could result in delays or even confiscation. By following these guidelines, you can ensure that bringing your medication into Jamaica goes smoothly and without issue.

Penalties

Marijuana

As mentioned above, the penalties for marijuana possession in Jamaica vary depending on the amount and the situation. For small amounts—up to 2 ounces—the law is more lenient. Possessing this quantity for personal use is considered a **ticketable offense** rather than a criminal one. In such cases, you might receive a fine or be given a notice to appear in court, but you won't face jail time. This applies to both locals and tourists, reflecting the country's more relaxed stance on small-scale possession.

However, if you're caught with more than 2 ounces, the situation becomes much more serious. Possession of larger quantities is treated as a **criminal offense**, and the penalties can include imprisonment. Depending on how much you have, you could face up to 5 years in prison. If authorities believe you're involved in selling or trafficking marijuana, the consequences are even more severe, with possible sentences of 10 years or more behind bars, along with hefty fines.

Growing marijuana is allowed for personal use, but there are limits—up to 5 plants—and exceeding this amount can lead to criminal charges as well. So, while Jamaica has decriminalized small-scale possession for personal use, possessing larger amounts or being involved in trafficking could land you in serious legal trouble. It's important to stay aware of the laws to avoid any unwanted consequences during your visit.

Illicit Drugs

In Jamaica, the penalties for possessing other illegal drugs—such as **cocaine, heroin, methamphetamine**, and **ecstasy**—are strict and can result in severe consequences. Unlike marijuana, which has been decriminalized for small amounts, drugs like these are considered dangerous and their possession is treated with zero tolerance.

If you're caught with any illegal drugs, regardless of the amount, you could face serious charges. The penalties can range from heavy fines to lengthy prison sentences, depending on the type and quantity of the drug. For example, being caught with even small amounts of cocaine or heroin can lead to several years in prison, and trafficking or attempting to smuggle these drugs into the country can result in much harsher penalties, including life imprisonment.

Drug trafficking is considered a major crime, and those involved in the distribution or transportation of illegal substances face long sentences, often upwards of 25 years in prison, with the possibility of life sentences for larger quantities. This includes both local and international trafficking. Even possessing drug paraphernalia or being caught under the influence of illegal drugs can result in significant fines and jail time.

Jamaican authorities maintain a strong stance against drugs, with strict enforcement of laws to combat the illegal drug trade. As a result, it's essential to avoid any involvement with illegal drugs while visiting the country. The penalties are severe, and the risk of legal trouble is high.

Prescription Medication

If you're caught with prescription medications and fail to provide the necessary documents, you could face severe penalties, including fines or imprisonment. The severity of the penalty depends on the type and quantity of the medication. For instance, narcotics or other controlled drugs are treated as illegal substances and possessing them without the correct paperwork may result in being charged with drug possession.

For larger quantities or if authorities suspect you're intending to distribute the medications, the penalties could be even harsher, including long prison sentences. Therefore, it's crucial to ensure that your medications are clearly labeled, accompanied by the appropriate documentation, and in reasonable quantities for personal use to avoid running into legal issues while traveling in Jamaica.

General Questions

1. *Is cannabis legal in Jamaica?* Yes. Marijuana is legal in Jamaica in quantities no greater than two ounces for medical purposes, for scientific or therapeutic purposes in licensed businesses, or for persons with doctor's notes. It is still illegal to possess large quantities of marijuana.

2. *Where can I legally purchase marijuana in Jamaica?* In Jamaica, marijuana can be legally purchased from businesses licensed by the Cannabis Licensing Authority, which is responsible for regulating its sale. Currently, 15 licensed establishments offer marijuana for medical or therapeutic purposes. For more details on navigating marijuana purchase in Jamaica, you can visit the following websites:

   https://www.forbes.com/sites/mikeadams/2018/05/03/toker-travels-how-to-buy-marijuana-legally-in-jamaica/#7ed3d38f38df

https://www.itopialife.com/

http://epican.com/

https://kayaherbhouse.com/

3. *Besides carrying cannabis for personal use, can I have marijuana in my hotel room or villa?* Although the law related to cannabis does not reference hotel rooms or villas for tourists, it does state that each household in Jamaica may grow up to five cannabis plants.

4. *Are there any other exceptions to the possession and consumption of cannabis in Jamaica?* No. Besides the exceptions referenced above, it remains illegal for persons to possess over two ounces of marijuana. Violators can be fined, jailed, sentenced, and imprisoned for a period and may sustain a criminal arrest record.

5. *What are the penalties for possessing and consuming other types of illicit drugs in Jamaica?* Judges in Jamaica have the discretion to punish those convicted of drug charges with moderate to severe jail sentences based on sentencing guidelines. In addition, Jamaica has taken a harsher approach to penalize those people charged with drug possession.

 **Law of the Land Hypothetical**

HYPOTHETICAL 1: *The police stop Larry in Jamaica. He has less than two ounces of cannabis. Larry is not sure if police will arrest him or issue a civil fine for possessing cannabis. He is concerned that the government will deport him and not allow him to re-enter Jamaica on a future visit. What is the likely result?*

ANSWER: *Larry should not worry about criminal sanctions or civil sanctions for carrying less than two ounces of cannabis in Jamaica. Under current law, marijuana is legal in Jamaica in quantities no* greater than two ounces for medical purposes, for scientific or thera-peutic purposes in licensed businesses, or for people with a prescription. But it is still a violation of the law to carry large quantities of cannabis in Jamaica for personal or commercial purposes.

HYPOTHETICAL 2: *The next day, Jamaican police stop Larry again with a small quantity of cocaine. They weigh the cocaine and determine that it weighs less than two ounces. Larry remembers that he could carry up to two ounces of marijuana in Jamaica with no major legal reper-cussions. Larry hopes there are similar allowances for possession of cocaine. Is Larry going to be criminally liable?*

ANSWER: *Yes. There are no allowances for possession of any other drugs in Jamaica. Any quantity is illegal to possess in Jamaica and the judge may punish a defendant for possessing any amount.*

Takeaways

- It is legal to carry less than two ounces of marijuana if there is a medical or scientific purpose and you carry a prescription.
- It is illegal to carry large quantities of marijuana for commercial purposes.
- It is illegal to possess other types of illicit drugs in Jamaica includ-ing, but not limited, to drugs like cocaine and heroin.

ALCOHOL-RELATED OFFENSES

IN THIS CHAPTER

- Alcohol-Related Offenses
- Alcohol Regulations
- General Questions
- Law of the Land Hypothetical

ALCOHOL-RELATED OFFENSES

Alcohol-Related Offenses

In Jamaica, alcohol, especially rum, has deep historical roots dating back to the colonial era when it was produced from sugarcane. Over time, it became a symbol of Jamaican identity. Culturally, alcohol is a key part of social gatherings, celebrations, and communal events and is also used in traditional rituals, especially in Rastafari practices. It is commonly enjoyed during family gatherings, parties, celebrations, and festivals. Sharing drinks with friends and family is a way of bonding, and alcohol is often present at casual meetups, barbecues, and beach outings. It also plays a central role in Jamaica's tourism industry, with visitors enjoying local beverages during their stay.

Alcohol is legal and widely available in Jamaica and can be purchased at bars, restaurants, grocery stores, and liquor shops across the island. The legal drinking age in Jamaica is 18; you may be asked for ID when buying alcohol, especially if you're in a more formal setting like a bar or a nightclub. While it might not be as strictly enforced in casual settings or smaller shops, it's always a good idea to carry identification if you plan to purchase alcohol.

Popular drinks include **rum** (often enjoyed neat or in cocktails like **Rum Punch**), **Red Stripe beer**, and **Ting with rum**, a refreshing grapefruit soda mixed with rum. **Jamaican Sorrel Drink**, made from sorrel petals and sometimes spiked with rum, is especially popular during the holidays.

The National Council on Drug Abuse (NCDA) recently conducted a comprehensive Household Drug Survey, shedding light on the prevalent patterns of alcohol consumption in Jamaica. The findings reveal a substantial prevalence, indicating that a significant portion of the population engages in drinking habits, with a notable 40% of the Jamaican population reported being consumers of alcohol. This statistic underscores the widespread nature of alcohol consumption across the country. It reflects the cultural significance and social acceptance of alcohol within the Jamaican community.

Alcohol Regulation

It's important for residents and visitors alike to be aware of the cultural norms, legal regulations, and potential consequences associated with alcohol use in Jamaica. In Jamaica, alcohol regulations are governed by a combination of local laws and policies that aim to regulate the production, sale, and consumption of alcoholic beverages. Some key points include:

- **Legal Drinking Age:** The legal drinking age in Jamaica is 18 years old. Anyone under this age is prohibited from purchasing or consuming alcohol.
- **Alcohol Sales Hours:** Alcohol can generally be sold during normal business hours, but there are restrictions on sales during certain times, such as holidays or special events when extended hours may be allowed. Some areas may have specific laws regarding the hours during which alcohol can be sold.
- **Licensing:** To legally sell alcohol, businesses (such as bars, restaurants, and liquor stores) must be properly licensed by the Jamaican government. There are strict regulations for issuing liquor licenses.
- **Public Consumption:** Public drinking, particularly on the streets, is not illegal, but there are regulations in place to control where and

how alcohol is consumed in public spaces. It's more common to drink in designated areas like bars, restaurants, or private properties.

- **Drunk Driving:** Like most countries, Jamaica has laws against driving under the influence. The blood alcohol concentration (BAC) limit for drivers is 0.08%, and violations can lead to hefty fines, license suspension, or even imprisonment.

- **Alcohol Advertising:** Alcohol advertisements are regulated, and there are restrictions on advertising targeted at minors. Ads must adhere to ethical standards, promoting responsible drinking.

- **Restrictions on Minors:** Minors under 18 are prohibited from purchasing alcohol, and businesses can face penalties for selling alcohol to underage individuals.

 **General Questions**

6. *I am only 18 years old. Will I get in trouble for possessing an open container of alcohol in public?* No. The legal age to consume alcohol in Jamaica is 18 years old. There are no restrictions under the law for drinking alcoholic beverages in public. Private establishments may set their own rules or guidelines. However, police rarely enforce alcohol consumption laws.

7. *Can I drink and drive in Jamaica?* No, drinking and driving is illegal in Jamaica. The legal blood alcohol concentration (BAC) limit is 0.08%, and if you exceed this limit, you can face serious consequences. These include hefty fines, potential license suspension, and even imprisonment. It's important to always drink responsibly and use alternative transportation (like taxis or ride-sharing services) if you plan to consume alcoholic beverages.

 **Law of the Land Hypothetical**

HYPOTHETICAL 1: *Henry was drinking and walking on a public sidewalk with an open container of alcohol. Later that day, he rented a car and drove around Kingston with a blood alcohol level of .09%. Is Henry violating any laws for his activities in Jamaica?*

ANSWER: *Henry is not violating any laws for carrying an open container of alcohol. However, he is violating criminal traffic laws by driving with a blood alcohol level above .08%. Henry faces fines and imprisonment for driving under the influence.*

FIREARM & AMMUNITION OFFENSES

FIREARM & AMMUNITION OFFENSES

Current Firearm Status[5]

In Jamaica, the ownership of firearms is tightly regulated, with only certain individuals eligible to possess them legally. The Firearms Licensing Authority (FLA) oversees the process, ensuring that only those who can demonstrate a legitimate need are granted licenses. Typically, those who require firearms for professional or safety reasons, such as business owners, security personnel, or farmers dealing with threats to property or livestock, may apply for a license. Additionally, people in high-risk occupations, such as certain government officials or those in law enforcement, may also be authorized to carry firearms.

Firearms ownership for the average citizen is tightly controlled in Jamaica. The license application process is rigorous, and applicants must provide clear evidence that owning a firearm is necessary for their safety or profession. Before issuing a license, the FLA conducts thorough background checks, looking into the applicant's criminal history, financial stability, and even their mental health to ensure they are fit to own a weapon. There are also age requirements, and applicants must generally be at least 25 years old. Importantly, anyone with a history of violent crime or domestic abuse is excluded from firearm ownership.

---

5   https://fla.gov.jm/Resources/Firearms-Acts

Additionally, only certain types of firearms can be legally possessed by licensed individuals. These include handguns, shotguns, and rifles, which are typically used for personal protection, hunting, or agricultural purposes. The possession of automatic or semi-automatic firearms is generally restricted to law enforcement and military personnel, with civilians not permitted to own them under normal circumstances.

When it comes to possession limits, the law generally allows individuals to own one handgun and one long gun (such as a rifle or shotgun), provided they can justify the need for both. Ownership beyond this limit requires a clear, valid reason, and the Firearms Licensing Authority carefully monitors and regulates the number of firearms any individual can hold. All firearms must be registered, and the authority can revoke licenses if possession is deemed unnecessary or excessive. The process is designed to ensure firearms are kept in responsible hands and are used for legitimate purposes.

To carry a firearm in public in Jamaica, individuals must first obtain a valid license, demonstrating a legitimate need, such as personal protection or security work. Additionally, the applicant must complete required firearm safety training. Even with a license, firearms must be concealed and cannot be carried in restricted areas like government buildings or schools. Failing to comply with these regulations can result in severe penalties, including fines or imprisonment.

Restrictions on Visitors

Non-residents and visitors to Jamaica are not permitted to bring firearms into the country, whether for personal use or any other purpose. Jamaican firearm laws are very strict, and only authorized individuals with specific licenses are allowed to possess or carry firearms. Visitors found in possession of a firearm without proper authorization can face serious legal consequences, including arrest and imprisonment.

If a non-resident wishes to bring a firearm into Jamaica, they will need to follow a very stringent process and obtain approval in advance, which is generally only granted under specific circumstances, such as for certain professional or sporting events. However, for typical tourists, firearms are prohibited, and it is advised to adhere to the country's laws regarding weapons.

 For more information on traveling with firearms, visit **https://www.atf.gov/firearms/traveling-firearms**.

 **Penalties**

Penalties for some firearm crimes are as follows:

- **Possession of an illegal firearm:** If someone is found in possession of an unlicensed firearm, they can face up to 15 years in prison. This includes both illegal firearms and ammunition.

- **Carrying a firearm without a license:** Anyone caught carrying a firearm without the proper license can be charged and face imprisonment for up to 15 years.

- **Unlawful use of a firearm:** If a firearm is used in the commission of a crime, such as in a robbery or shooting, the penalties are even harsher, with life imprisonment being a possible sentence.

- **Illegal importation or exportation of firearms:** Attempting to smuggle firearms into or out of Jamaica without proper authorization can lead to a lengthy prison sentence.

- **Possession of ammunition without a license:** Being found in possession of ammunition without a valid license also carries severe penalties, including potential prison time.

General Questions

1. *What happens if the police catch me carrying a firearm?*
Possession of firearms and ammunition in Jamaica is illegal and can carry heavy fines and prison sentences.

2. *What is a potential sentence for a firearms violation upon conviction?* In Jamaica, firearms violations carry severe penalties upon conviction. Possessing an unlicensed firearm or ammunition can lead to up to 15 years in prison. Carrying a firearm without the proper license also carries a sentence of up to 15 years. If a firearm is used in the commission of a crime, such as a robbery, the penalty can be much more severe, with life imprisonment being a potential outcome. Those convicted of smuggling firearms into or out of Jamaica face long prison sentences, often up to 20 years or more. These strict laws reflect Jamaica's commitment to tackling gun violence and maintaining public safety.

Law of the Land Hypothetical

HYPOTHETICAL: *Stephen brought a firearm in his checked luggage from the United States into Jamaica. He is looking to have a fun and safe time with his family in Jamaica, and while does not intend to use the firearm, he brought it for his protection. Stephen has a concealed weapons permit from Florida. If the police stop Stephen, will the Florida permit be valid in Jamaica?*

ANSWER: *No, Stephen's Florida concealed weapons permit will not be valid in Jamaica. Jamaica has strict gun control laws, and a concealed weapons permit from another country, including the U.S., does not grant permission to carry a firearm in Jamaica. Visitors are not allowed to bring firearms into the country unless they have obtained a specific license issued by the Jamaican government, which is difficult to obtain. Anyone caught with a firearm in Jamaica without the* proper permit can face severe legal penalties, including imprisonment. Therefore, even if Stephen holds a valid concealed carry permit in Florida, it will not provide any legal protection if he attempts to carry a weapon in Jamaica.

 ## Law of the Land True Story

A U.S. military veteran was arrested after unknowingly carrying ammunition in his luggage, despite not having a firearm. While passing through Montego Bay's airport, a screener discovered a hidden shotgun shell at the bottom of his swim bag. The veteran and his wife were unaware that it had been there the entire week, having slipped through airport security multiple times during their travels to the island. After being detained for three days, the veteran was eventually released.

 ## Takeaways

- Jamaica has stringent laws governing firearm ownership, allowing only individuals with legitimate professional or safety needs to apply for a license.

- Possessing an unlicensed firearm, carrying a firearm without a license, or using a firearm in the commission of a crime can lead to severe penalties, including up to 15 years in prison. Illegal importation or possession of ammunition is also heavily penalized.

- Non-residents and tourists are prohibited from bringing firearms into Jamaica.

- Even an unintentional violation can result in arrest and detainment.

- A foreign concealed carry permit is not valid in Jamaica. Visitors are not allowed to carry firearms unless they have received approval from Jamaican authorities, and violating this law can lead to serious legal repercussions.

CHAPTER 7

PROSTITUTION

IN THIS CHAPTER

- Overview
- Laws and Penalties
- Prostitution Practices
- Sex Trafficking and Exploitation
- Sex Tourism and Public Health
- Tips to Avoid Being Solicited
- Law of the Land Hypothetical
- Takeaways

PROSTITUTION

Overview[6]

Prostitution in Jamaica is illegal, and there are no specific regulations or legal frameworks in place to govern it. Engaging in, soliciting, or profiting from prostitution is a criminal offense under Jamaican law. Despite its illegal status, prostitution is a known part of the informal economy in certain areas, particularly in tourist destinations like Montego Bay and Negril, where sex tourism is an ongoing issue.

Trends in prostitution often correlate with tourism, as many tourists—both domestic and international—participate in these activities. Some women and men engage in sex work voluntarily, while others, particularly minors or those living in extreme poverty, may be victims of exploitation. Prostitution often takes place in private homes, bars, clubs, or along beaches, and sometimes involves pimping and human trafficking, which are also illegal in Jamaica.

Authorities have attempted to crack down on prostitution, particularly with efforts to combat human trafficking and child prostitution, but challenges persist due to poverty, lack of employment opportunities, and the sex tourism industry. In some parts of the country, there is a lack of legal recourse for those involved in sex work, leaving many vulnerable individuals with limited support.

---

6   https://en.wikipedia.org/wiki/Prostitution_in_Jamaica

 **Laws and Penalties**

In Jamaica, sex work is criminalized under the Sexual Offences Act, the Offences Against the Person Act, and the Towns and Communities Act. Specific offenses include procuring someone to become a prostitute, living off the earnings of prostitution, and soliciting for immoral purposes. Penalties for these crimes can include up to 10 years in prison, a fine of up to $500,000, or both, depending on the offense.

While local sex workers are generally not targeted unless other crimes are involved (such as violence or theft), tourists may face penalties if caught engaging in sex work. Jamaican authorities also have the right to deny entry to individuals believed to be visiting the country for prostitution purposes.

Prostitution Practices

In Jamaica, female prostitutes typically solicit from their homes, hotel rooms, or private residences, with many working in adult nightclubs, especially in Kingston, which attract tourists, diplomats, and affluent locals. Some of these sex workers are from other countries and work in upscale clubs, while others are local women, including those with regular jobs. In Ocho Rios, sex workers may pay club owners a fee to use the premises to find clients. Massage parlors in Jamaica sometimes double as fronts for brothels, and some dancers in strip clubs offer sexual services. Gay prostitution exists, though it is less visible due to the country's homophobic tendencies, with male prostitutes often working discreetly. In tourist hotspots like Montego Bay and Ocho Rios, sex workers may try to form connections with tourists, offering sexual favors in exchange for the chance to travel abroad.

The approach to sex work in Jamaica is a mix of criminalization, selective enforcement, and tolerance. Even though prostitution is illegal in Jamaica, it remains widely accepted, particularly in tourist areas where it has become a significant aspect of the local economy. According to

UNAIDS, there are close to 19,000 prostitutes in the country, which illustrates the prevalence of sexual service transactions despite legal prohibitions.[7]

Sex Trafficking and Exploitation

Sex trafficking and exploitation are significant concerns in Jamaica, largely due to its role as a major tourist destination and its challenges with poverty, limited economic opportunities, and socio-economic inequality. These factors create vulnerabilities that traffickers often exploit, targeting mostly women and children for sexual exploitation.

Jamaica's large tourist industry, particularly in areas like Montego Bay, Negril, and Ocho Rios, provides a market for both legal and illegal sex work. Some tourists and local clients contribute to demand for sexual services, and traffickers take advantage of this demand by coercing or deceiving victims, often under false promises of employment or a better life. Many victims are lured with promises of legitimate jobs in the tourism sector or are recruited from impoverished communities, only to find themselves trapped in exploitative conditions.

The Jamaican government has made several efforts to combat human trafficking and sexual exploitation, primarily through legislation like the Trafficking in Persons Act and the creation of the National Task Force Against Trafficking in Persons (NATFATIP). These initiatives aim to strengthen law enforcement, increase public awareness, and provide victim support through shelters and legal aid. The government has also worked to improve training for officials and collaborated internationally to tackle trafficking.

While the government has taken steps to combat trafficking and exploitation, limited resources, corruption, and a lack of victim support systems can hinder effective prevention and prosecution efforts. Vulnerable populations, including minors, are often the most at risk, and cases of child sex trafficking have been reported.

---

7   https://en.wikipedia.org/wiki/Prostitution_in_Jamaica

International organizations, such as the U.S. State Department, have raised concerns about the scale of sex trafficking in Jamaica, noting that both domestic and international trafficking networks are active within the country. The Jamaican government has made efforts to address trafficking, but the problem remains a significant challenge due to its complex socio-economic and cultural underpinnings.

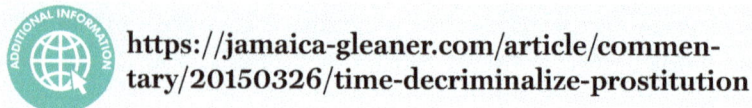

https://jamaica-gleaner.com/article/commentary/20150326/time-decriminalize-prostitution

Sex Tourism and Public Health

In Jamaica, sex tourism is most prominent in areas with heavy tourist traffic and vibrant nightlife. Montego Bay, Negril, Ocho Rios, and Kingston are the main destinations where sex tourism can be observed. Montego Bay, a major tourist hub, is known for its bustling nightlife and some bars and clubs that cater to adult entertainment. Negril, famous for its relaxed beach vibe, attracts tourists looking for both leisure and excitement, and some parts of the town have ties to sex tourism. Ocho Rios, while less overt, still has a noticeable presence due to its mix of tourism and nightlife. Kingston, the capital, offers a more upscale sex tourism scene, often linked to international visitors, diplomats, and businesspeople. In all these areas, the combination of tourism, clubs, and adult services creates environments where sex tourism thrives, despite ongoing government efforts to address the issue.

Sex tourism in Jamaica is not officially advertised, but it exists through informal networks and is facilitated in areas with heavy tourist traffic. It often operates through word of mouth, connections with local taxi drivers or hotel staff, and in venues like nightclubs, bars, massage parlors, and strip clubs, where sex workers may offer services alongside entertainment. Some sex workers advertise their services through classified ads or online platforms, and private arrangements are commonly made in hotel rooms or private homes. While the Jamaican government has made efforts to combat these activities, sex tourism remains an ongoing concern, particularly in tourist-heavy regions.

 Sex tourism and prostitution in Jamaica raise significant public health concerns, primarily related to the transmission of sexually transmitted infections (STIs), including HIV. The concentration of sex workers in popular tourist areas increases the risk of exposure to these infections, both among tourists and the local population. The informal nature of much of the sex trade means that many workers are not provided with adequate health services or education on safe practices. Additionally, a lack of consistent condom use, especially among those working in high-demand tourism sectors, heightens the risk of STIs. Despite efforts by the government and NGOs to provide STI education and support, gaps remain in reaching the more vulnerable groups involved in sex work, particularly those working outside formal channels, like street-based sex workers or those in informal establishments. This creates a cycle where health risks are not adequately addressed, increasing the spread of infections in communities.

 ## Tips to Avoid Being Solicited

To avoid being solicited by sex workers in Jamaica, here are a few practical tips:

- Choose accommodations in well-known, reputable areas like resorts or hotels that are not located in high-risk zones for sex tourism. Avoid wandering into less secure neighborhoods, especially at night.

- Avoid engaging in conversations or giving signals that could be misinterpreted as interest. If approached, respond politely but firmly and move on without engaging.

- Stay in well-populated areas, particularly in tourist-friendly zones, and avoid walking alone in quiet or poorly lit areas, especially after dark.

- Be cautious about entering establishments like strip clubs, massage parlors, or bars that seem to cater specifically to tourists or have a reputation for illicit activities.

- Be aware that prostitution is illegal in Jamaica, and engaging in such activities could have serious legal consequences. Stick to legal, regulated activities during your stay.

 **Law of the Land Hypothetical**

HYPOTHETICAL: *Jim and Mary are in an open marriage and often travel to Jamaica, where they engage in sexual activities with local individuals, both men and women, whom they pay for sex. Are Jim and Mary breaking any laws by engaging in paid sexual encounters with locals during their trips to Jamaica?*

ANSWER: *While prostitution is illegal in Jamaica, it's often tolerated in tourist areas, so they might not face immediate legal issues locally. However, if their activities involve exploitation or trafficking, they could be violating more serious laws. Additionally, depending on their home country, they might also face legal trouble under laws that prohibit sex tourism or extraterritorial laws against prostitution abroad, particularly if there's any coercion involved.*

Takeaways

Some key takeaways regarding prostitution and sex work in Jamaica include:

- Prostitution is illegal in Jamaica, and various laws criminalize activities such as solicitation, living off earnings from prostitution, and procuring someone for sex work.

- While prostitution is illegal, it is still prevalent in popular tourist destinations like Negril, Montego Bay, and Kingston, often in the form of street solicitation or through nightclubs and massage parlors.

- Law enforcement typically does not target tourists or locals involved in sex work unless other crimes, like violence, are also involved.

- Jamaica has struggled with human trafficking and the exploitation of women and children in the sex industry.

- Sex work is associated with public health risks, such as the transmission of STIs, including HIV.

- Jamaica has immigration laws that allow officials to deny entry to anyone suspected of coming to the country for prostitution purposes, emphasizing the government's stance against sex tourism.

LGBTQ

IN THIS CHAPTER

- Homophobia in Jamaica
- LGBTQ Legislation
- LGBTQ Tourism and Safety Concerns
- General Questions
- Law of the Land Hypothetical
- Law of the Land True Story

CHAPTER 8

LGBTQ

Homophobia in Jamaica

Homophobia remains a significant issue in Jamaica, both within society and in terms of government attitudes toward the LGBTQ+ community. Jamaica has one of the most homophobic cultures in the Caribbean, with both legal and social challenges faced by individuals identifying as LGBTQ+.

LGBTQ+ individuals face widespread discrimination, stigmatization, and violence. Homophobic sentiments are often deeply ingrained in the cultural and religious fabric of the nation, with many religious groups, particularly Christian denominations, condemning same-sex relationships. Public attitudes can be harsh, with LGBTQ+ individuals facing physical and verbal abuse, including "corrective rape" aimed at changing their sexual orientation. Openly gay and lesbian individuals are at risk, as incidents of assault, harassment, and, tragically, murders targeting the LGBTQ community are regrettably common. The issue extends beyond mere societal attitudes, with even some popular Jamaican music entertainers incorporating anti-homosexual messages and endorsing violence against LGBTQ individuals in their song lyrics.

Public figures who are openly LGBTQ+ or who express pro-LGBTQ+ views often face backlash, and LGBTQ+ pride events, such as pride parades, are unlikely to be openly celebrated without significant risk. However, there have been small signs of progress, especially in urban areas and within certain advocacy circles. International pressure, including from human rights organizations, has raised awareness of the LGBTQ+ community's struggles, and some organizations in Jamaica have been working to provide support and create safer spaces for LGBTQ+ individuals.

LGBTQ Legislation

The Jamaican government has been slow to embrace changes in LGBTQ+ rights. Homosexuality is criminalized under the Offences Against the Person Act, which has been in place since colonial time, prohibiting "buggery," which includes consensual anal sex between men. This law applies to both homosexual and heterosexual acts, though it predominantly affects men. The penalties for engaging in same-sex sexual acts can include up to 10 years in prison with hard labor. Additionally, "gross indecency," which refers to other sexual acts between men (such as oral sex), is also prohibited under the law, and can lead to imprisonment for up to 2 years.

In 2011, the Jamaican Parliament passed the Charter of Fundamental Rights and Freedoms (Constitutional Amendment) Act, which explicitly bans same-sex marriage and any other kind of union between same-sex couples to be recognized in Jamaica. Additionally, transgender people are not allowed to change their gender in Jamaica as a person's gender identity is not legally recognized in Jamaica. For all official purposes, gender assigned at birth overrules gender identity.

Attitudes toward LGBTQ+ individuals do vary somewhat by location. Urban areas like Kingston, Montego Bay, and Negril tend to be more tolerant, especially due to tourism and exposure to international visitors. Kingston, for example, has a small LGBTQ+ community and some advocacy groups, while Negril offers a more laid-back, tourist-friendly atmosphere. However, rural areas and more conservative parishes remain less accepting, influenced by traditional values and religious beliefs. In these areas, LGBTQ+ individuals may face hostility, discrimination, and even violence.

While there has been some advocacy for reform, the government has been resistant to change, fearing backlash from religious groups and conservative segments of the population. There are currently no comprehensive legal protections against discrimination for LGBTQ+ individuals in Jamaica. While the country has some anti-discrimination laws in place, such as those related to employment, they do not explicitly include sexual orientation or gender identity as protected categories. As a result, LGBTQ+ people in Jamaica are vulnerable to discrimination in various areas, including employment, housing, healthcare, and public accommodations.

LGBTQ Tourism and Safety Concerns

LGBTQ+ tourism in Jamaica is a nuanced subject due to the country's conservative stance on LGBTQ+ issues. While homosexuality remains a sensitive topic in Jamaican society, a number of LGBTQ+ travelers still visit the island, drawn by its natural beauty, rich culture, and vibrant tourism industry.

Jamaica's tourism industry has begun to recognize the market potential of LGBTQ+ visitors, though much of this tourism tends to be discreet. Areas like Negril, Montego Bay, and parts of Kingston are known for being somewhat more tolerant due to the international tourist presence, with some hotels and resorts catering to LGBTQ+ clients. Negril, in particular, has a reputation for being more laid-back and accepting, with certain private resorts and boutique hotels offering LGBTQ+-friendly environments. The island's tourism sector is aware of LGBTQ+ travel trends, and there are private accommodations, events, and cruise excursions tailored to these visitors, allowing them to enjoy the island without feeling exposed. However, it is important to note that such establishments generally prefer to operate discreetly due to the sensitive nature of the subject in the wider Jamaican society.

LGBTQ travelers to Jamaica should take a thoughtful and respectful approach due to the island's conservative cultural values. To ensure safety and comfort, it's recommended to limit public displays of affection, dress conservatively to avoid unwanted attention, and research

LGBTQ-friendly venues and accommodations. Connecting with local LGBTQ communities or organizations can provide insights into safe spaces and help navigate potential challenges. Travelers should also stay informed about local laws regarding LGBTQ rights, be mindful of their surroundings, and consider participating in quieter activities. Engaging with locals for guidance on safe and welcoming places can enhance the travel experience while maintaining cultural sensitivity.

 ## General Questions

1. *Do laws in Jamaica protect homosexual expressions and conduct?* Laws in Jamaica do not provide legal protection for homosexual expressions and conduct. In fact, same-sex sexual acts between consenting adults remain criminalized under the country's laws, specifically sections of the Offences Against the Person Act. This includes "buggery" (anal sex) and "gross indecency," which can result in penalties such as imprisonment.

2. *What is the punishment for homosexual expressions and conduct?* In Jamaica, homosexual conduct, including buggery and gross indecency, is criminalized under the Offences Against the Person Act, with penalties of up to 10 years in prison for buggery and up to 2 years for gross indecency. These laws contribute to the country's legal and social environment that remains hostile towards LGBTQ+ individuals.

 ## Law of the Land Hypothetical

HYPOTHETICAL: *Benjamin and his boyfriend, Nicholas, are planning a summer trip to Jamaica and want to make sure their stay is enjoyable*

and safe. What advice would be helpful for them to consider before traveling to Jamaica?

ANSWER: *Benjamin and Nicholas should be mindful of Jamaica's conservative views on LGBTQ+ issues and exercise discretion in public, especially outside major tourist areas. Staying at LGBTQ+-friendly accommodations in places like Montego Bay or Negril is recommended for a more welcoming environment. They should also avoid public displays of affection and be aware of the legal landscape, as homosexuality remains illegal in Jamaica, though enforcement is generally not targeted at tourists. Finally, exercising caution and being informed about their surroundings will help ensure a safe and enjoyable trip.*

Law of the Land True Story

Gareth Henry, a well-known LGBTQ rights advocate in Jamaica, was forced to seek asylum in Canada after enduring severe persecution due to his sexual orientation and activism. As a vocal supporter for LGBTQ rights, Gareth faced threats, violence, and harassment in Jamaica, largely fueled by the country's laws that criminalize consensual same-sex intimacy between adult men. These laws created a hostile environment, leaving LGBTQ individuals vulnerable to societal discrimination and physical harm, with little to no state protection.

Gareth's asylum claim in Canada was based on the argument that Jamaican laws, which criminalize private, consensual sexual acts, directly contributed to the persecution he faced. His case became a landmark legal battle, leading to a ruling that these laws violated Jamaica's obligations under the American Convention on Human Rights. This decision was a powerful challenge to the discriminatory legal framework in Jamaica and highlighted the broader global struggle for LGBTQ rights.

Although Gareth's successful asylum case was a personal victory, it also brought international attention to the ongoing discrimination faced by LGBTQ individuals in Jamaica. His journey underscores the need for continued advocacy, legal reforms, and greater protection for the rights of LGBTQ people, both within Jamaica and globally.

 Additional information on LGBTQ communities and organizations in Jamaica can be found at the following link: **https://www.rainbowgetaways.net/post/ can-you-be-gay-in-jamaica**

 Additional information about LGBTQ-friendly establish-ments in Jamaica can be found at the following links: **https://www.misterbandb.com/gay-guide/jamaica** and **https://www.thetravel.com/ lgbtq-friendly-hotels-in-jamaica/**.

CHAPTER 9

SEXUALLY MOTIVATED/ VIOLENT CRIMES

SEXUALLY MOTIVATED/ VIOLENT CRIMES

Overview[8]

Sexually motivated crimes, including sexual assault and rape, are indeed a concern in Jamaica. The country struggles with high rates of gender-based violence, including incidents of sexual violence against women and children. Reports indicate that sexual crimes, such as rape and sexual harassment, are often underreported due to societal stigma, fear of retaliation, and mistrust in the legal system. In many cases, perpetrators of sexual violence face minimal consequences, contributing to a culture of impunity.

There are also issues with "revenge porn" and exploitation, where individuals, especially women and minors, can become victims of sexual abuse. Although there are laws in place to address sexual crimes, such as the Sexual Offences Act, enforcement and accountability remain challenges, and many survivors face obstacles to justice. In addition, sexual violence can intersect with other forms of violence, such as domestic abuse. Awareness campaigns and advocacy for stronger legal protections and improved support for survivors are ongoing, but societal attitudes,

---

8   https://www.wkyc.com/article/news/nation-world/its-not-just-jamaica-these-caribbean-islands-also-have-major-sex-crimes-problems/507-609937910

lack of resources, and cultural norms still present significant barriers to tackling sexually motivated crimes effectively.

In Jamaica, sexual violence primarily affects women, girls, and children, with women being the most frequent victims of rape, sexual assault, and domestic violence. Children, especially girls, face a high incidence of sexual abuse, often within the family or by trusted individuals. LGBTQ+ individuals, particularly gay men and transgender people, are also at a heightened risk due to societal homophobia and discrimination. Additionally, women in vulnerable situations, such as those involved in sex work or living in abusive domestic environments, are more likely to experience sexual violence. Domestic violence often includes sexual abuse, particularly within intimate partner relationships. While the majority of victims are locals, female tourists in certain areas may also face risks, particularly in regions associated with sex tourism.

While reliable and up-to-date statistics may vary due to underreporting and variations in law enforcement reporting, some key figures and trends offer insight into the prevalence of sexual violence in the country:

- **Rape and Sexual Offenses:** According to the Jamaican Constabulary Force (JCF), approximately 1,200 to 1,500 cases of rape are reported annually. However, it is believed that the actual number of rape cases may be much higher due to underreporting, cultural stigma, and fear of retaliation. Many victims, particularly women and children, may not come forward due to societal taboos or mistrust of the justice system.

- **Child Sexual Abuse:** Children, especially girls, are disproportionately affected by sexual violence in Jamaica. The Office of the Children's Registry (OCR) reports that a significant portion of sexual offenses involves minors. In 2019, the OCR recorded approximately 700 cases of child sexual abuse, with the majority involving girls. Sexual abuse against minors remains a serious issue, with many victims experiencing ongoing trauma.

- **Sexual Harassment:** While specific statistics on sexual harassment are difficult to track, it is known to be widespread, particularly in workplaces and schools. Surveys indicate that a high number of women in Jamaica have experienced sexual harassment, either verbal or physical, and that many do not report these incidents due to fear of retaliation or lack of legal protection.

- **Gender-Based Violence:** Gender-based violence (GBV) is a broader issue that encompasses sexual violence. The Jamaica Women's Health Survey has found that about 1 in 4 women report having experienced physical or sexual violence in their lifetime, with intimate partner violence being a common context. Gender-based violence, which includes sexual offenses, is one of the most pervasive forms of abuse in Jamaica.

- **Reports and Prosecution:** Despite the high number of reported incidents, Jamaica's conviction rates for sexual offenses are relatively low. This is often due to challenges such as delays in the justice system, insufficient evidence, and a lack of trust in law enforcement. According to the Jamaican Ministry of Justice, the conviction rate for sexual offenses remains troublingly low, indicating gaps in the judicial process for handling these cases effectively.

- **Domestic and Intimate Partner Sexual Violence:** Domestic violence, including sexual violence within intimate partnerships, is another area of concern. Data from the Ministry of National Security shows that intimate partner violence, including sexual abuse, constitutes a significant portion of the sexual offenses reported.

Related Legislation[9]

In Jamaica, several laws address sexually violent and sexually motivated crimes, although challenges remain in their enforcement and societal response. The Sexual Offences Act of 2009 is the primary piece of legislation governing sexual crimes in the country. This law defines and criminalizes a wide range of sexual offenses, including rape, sexual assault, incest, child sexual abuse, and sexual harassment. It stipulates severe penalties, with a sentence of up to life imprisonment for rape, and outlines penalties for other forms of sexual violence, including sexual assault and incest. The Offences Against the Person Act of 1864 also

---

9   https://caribbean.unwomen.org/en/caribbean-gender-portal/
    caribbean-gbv-law-portal/gbv-country-resources/jamaica

addresses sexual violence, covering crimes like unlawful carnal knowledge, historically referred to as rape. Though this law remains relevant, much of its language is outdated and lacks specificity in dealing with modern forms of sexual violence.

Additionally, the Domestic Violence Act of 1996 plays a crucial role in protecting individuals from sexual violence within intimate relationships, offering legal measures like protection orders for victims. The Child Care and Protection Act of 2004 further safeguards children, providing special provisions to prevent sexual abuse and exploitation, and holding caregivers accountable for the protection of minors. The Anti-Trafficking in Persons Act of 2007 targets sex trafficking, criminalizing the recruitment, transportation, and exploitation of individuals for sexual purposes, with heavy penalties for traffickers. Lastly, the Child Sexual Offences Act of 2004 focuses specifically on crimes involving minors, with heightened penalties for those convicted of sexually abusing children.

While these laws are robust, enforcement can be inconsistent, and societal attitudes, combined with a lack of resources for victims, often prevent many from seeking justice. These gaps, coupled with underreporting of sexual offenses, make the practical application of these laws challenging despite their existence.

Penalties

In Jamaica, penalties for sexually motivated and violent crimes are severe, reflecting the seriousness with which the law treats such offenses. The Sexual Offences Act outlines the following key penalties:

- **Rape:** A conviction for rape under the Sexual Offences Act can result in a sentence of up to life imprisonment, with the court having discretion to determine a fixed term based on the severity of the offense and the circumstances.

- **Sexual Assault:** Sexual assault, which includes unwanted touching or groping, is punishable by a prison sentence of up to 10 years. Aggravated sexual assault may attract a longer sentence.

- **Incest:** The law imposes a penalty of up to 20 years in prison for individuals convicted of incest, reflecting the grave nature of sexual abuse within families.

- **Child Sexual Abuse:** Offenders found guilty of sexually abusing a child may face life imprisonment, particularly if the child is under 12 years old. The Child Sexual Offences Act provides for these enhanced penalties.

- **Sexual Harassment:** Sexual harassment in a workplace or other social settings is punishable by a fine or imprisonment for up to 3 years under the Sexual Offences Act.

- **Trafficking in Persons:** Under the Anti-Trafficking in Persons Act (2007), individuals convicted of trafficking people for sexual exploitation face penalties of up to 20 years in prison, along with fines.

- **Unlawful Carnal Knowledge:** Under the Offences Against the Person Act (1864), unlawful carnal knowledge, typically understood as rape in modern terms, carries a maximum sentence of life imprisonment.

In addition to these specific penalties, the Jamaican legal system allows for fines, restraining orders, and other forms of restitution in cases involving sexual violence, particularly if the victim has suffered physical or psychological harm. Penalties may be aggravated if the victim is a child, or if the offender has a history of sexual violence. Although these penalties are meant to deter sexual violence, enforcement can be inconsistent, and societal attitudes may also complicate the prosecution of such crimes.

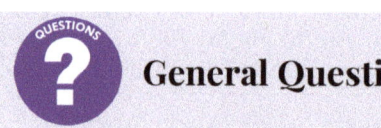

General Questions

1. ***Do laws in Jamaica related to sex crimes protect males and females equally?*** Jamaican laws related to sex crimes, such as the Sexual Offences Act, provide equal protection for both male and female victims, criminalizing sexual violence regardless of gender. However, societal attitudes and gender stereotypes sometimes create barriers for male victims, with underreporting and stigma affecting their access to justice. While the laws are gender-neutral, cultural challenges persist in fully ensuring equality in practice.

2. ***Pursuant to law, what is the age of consent for sex in Jamaica?*** The age of consent for sex in Jamaica is 16 years old, as outlined in the Sexual Offences Act. This means that individuals who are 16 years or older can legally engage in sexual activity, provided the encounter is consensual. However, there are additional provisions that protect minors, particularly regarding the age difference between partners, as laws are stricter if one party is in a position of trust or authority over the other, such as a teacher or employer.

Law of the Land Hypothetical

HYPOTHETICAL: *Craig and Samantha were victims of sex crimes during their visit to Jamaica. What rights as victims of such a crime do both Craig and Samantha have? What assistance can they receive?*

ANSWER: *In Jamaica, rape is deemed a crime resulting from vaginal penetration. Thus, Samantha can work with prosecutors to pursue "rape" charges against the suspects. However, Craig must pursue "sexual assault" charges against his perpetrators.*

As victims of sex crimes in Jamaica, both Craig and Samantha have the right to report the crime to the police and seek justice. They are entitled to legal protection, including the right to be heard and to have their cases investigated thoroughly. Victims of sexual violence in Jamaica are also entitled to medical care, including treatment for sexually transmitted infections and trauma counseling. Additionally, they can access support through victim services provided by government agencies and NGOs, such as the Ministry of Justice's Victim Services Division. This service can offer counseling, legal support, and assistance in navigating the legal process.

 ## Takeaways

- Sexually motivated crimes, including rape, sexual assault, and harassment, are significant concerns in Jamaica, with underreporting being common due to societal stigma, fear of retaliation, and mistrust of the justice system.

- Women, girls, and children are most affected by sexual violence in Jamaica, with a high number of reported cases involving minors, particularly girls. Vulnerable groups, including women in sex work or domestic violence situations, also face heightened risks.

- The Sexual Offences Act, along with other related legislation like the Domestic Violence Act and the Child Care and Protection Act, provides the legal framework to address sexual violence. However, enforcement remains inconsistent, and societal attitudes often hinder the effective application of these laws.

- The penalties for sexually motivated and violent crimes in Jamaica are severe, including life imprisonment for rape, sexual abuse of children, and trafficking in persons. Despite these penalties, the conviction rates remain low, reflecting challenges in the judicial process and cultural barriers.

- Victims of sexual violence, including both locals and tourists, are entitled to legal protection, medical care, and access to victim services, such as counseling and legal assistance. However, the accessibility and effectiveness of these services can be hindered by systemic barriers, underreporting, and limited resources for support.

ARRESTED IN JAMAICA

ARRESTED IN JAMAICA

Overview

When traveling in a foreign country, it is imperative to recognize that you are subject to the legal jurisdiction and regulations of that country. These laws may significantly differ from those in your home country and might not offer the same legal protections you are accustomed to. It is crucial to bear in mind that penalties for violating foreign laws can be more severe than those for similar offenses in your home country, and ignorance of these laws is not typically accepted as a defense.

The consequences for breaking the law while abroad can be severe and may include expulsion, fines, arrest or imprisonment. Even unintentional violations can lead to serious legal repercussions. It is essential for travelers to be aware of and adhere to the laws of the host country to avoid legal entanglements and ensure a safe and enjoyable experience.

Specifically, stringent penalties are often enforced for possession, use or trafficking of illegal drugs in many countries. Convicted offenders can expect severe consequences, including lengthy jail sentences and hefty fines. The legal processes for foreigners in the event of an arrest abroad involve being charged or indicted, prosecuted, potentially convicted and sentenced, and, if applicable, going through an appeals process.

Navigating a foreign legal system can be complex, and individuals arrested abroad must be prepared to comply with the legal procedures of the host country. Seeking legal representation and understanding the local legal nuances are crucial steps for those facing legal issues in a foreign jurisdiction.

Arrest Process

Visitors to Jamaica often find themselves in legal trouble for a few common offenses. One of the most frequent issues is drug possession, especially for illegal substances like cocaine or heroin, which can lead to serious legal consequences. Public disorder is another common charge, with tourists sometimes arrested for disruptive behavior such as public drunkenness or fighting. Drunk driving is strictly enforced in Jamaica, and visitors caught with a blood alcohol content above the legal limit face hefty fines and possible jail time. Sexual offenses also lead to arrests, particularly for those involved in illegal sex work or engaging in inappropriate conduct. Finally, violations of immigration laws, such as overstaying a visa or attempting to work without proper authorization, can result in detention or deportation. It's important for travelers to be aware of these issues to avoid legal trouble during their visit.

If a police officer suspects someone of committing a crime, they may stop and question the individual. If they believe there is probable cause, they can arrest the person. For minor offenses, such as public disorder, the police may issue a warning or fine, but for more serious crimes, an arrest is made. For arrests involving foreign nationals, police will typically inform the individual of their rights in English, though language barriers can sometimes occur.

The arrested is then transported to a police station for processing. If they are not immediately taken to court, they may be detained for up to 24 hours before being formally charged. In the case of a more serious crime, this period could be extended, but they must be brought before a judge or magistrate within 48 hours. Depending on the severity of the charge, the individual may be eligible for bail (discussed below). If bail is not granted, the person remains in police custody until their hearing.

If not released on bail, the person will appear before a magistrate or a judge, depending on the offense. In Jamaica, serious cases are often heard in the Resident Magistrate's Court, while minor offenses might be heard in the Petty Sessions Court.

Rights of the Arrested Person

In Jamaica, individuals who are arrested are afforded several key legal protections, ensuring their rights are upheld throughout the process. Arrested individuals have the right to remain silent and are not compelled to self-incriminate. They are also entitled to legal counsel, and if they cannot afford one, the state provides representation. The Constitution guarantees the right to a fair trial, protection from unlawful detention, and the right to be informed of the charges against them.

In Jamaica, there are certain special considerations for individuals who may face unique challenges in the legal system, such as juveniles, foreigners, and individuals with disabilities.

For juveniles, Jamaican law requires that they be treated with special care and attention, in line with both international conventions and local regulations. The Child Care and Protection Act mandates that juveniles be detained separately from adults, and they are entitled to legal representation and a hearing in a child-friendly environment. Additionally, any sentence for minors must focus on rehabilitation rather than punishment, and the justice system encourages diversionary measures, such as counseling or community service, where appropriate.

Foreign nationals arrested in Jamaica also benefit from certain protections. They have the right to contact their embassy or consulate for assistance, which can help with legal representation and ensuring that their rights are respected. In cases where a foreigner is detained, the authorities typically notify the embassy as part of the standard protocol. However, while these provisions exist, foreign nationals may sometimes face additional challenges, such as language barriers or unfamiliarity with local laws and customs, which can make navigating the legal system more complex.

Getting Legal Assistance

In Jamaica, foreign detainees have the right to legal counsel, similar to Jamaican citizens, under the country's Constitution and legal framework. According to the Charter of Fundamental Rights and Freedoms (Section 16 of the Jamaican Constitution), individuals who are detained or arrested have the right to communicate with an attorney of their choice. If they cannot afford an attorney, they are entitled to legal assistance at the state's expense, provided that they meet the necessary criteria.

For foreign detainees, this means they can contact their embassy or consulate. Your home embassy or consulate can offer crucial support, such as legal guidance, translation services, and communication with family members. They can also visit the detained U.S. citizen in jail, help ensure that prison officials provide appropriate medical care, explain the local criminal justice and legal processes, and most importantly, connect you to local attorneys who speak English. However, bear in mind, their powers are limited, and they cannot get U.S. citizens out of jail, provide legal advice or represent U.S. citizens in court, serve as official interpreters or translators, nor can they pay your legal, medical, or other fees.

The United States maintains a diplomatic presence in Jamaica, primarily through the U.S. Embassy located in the capitol, Kingston:

U.S. Embassy Jamaica

142 Old Hope Road, Kingston 6, Jamaica
Phone (General Inquiries): +1 876-702-6000
Visa Information: +1 876-702-6424 (Visa questions)
U.S. Citizens Services: +1 876-702-6450)
General Inquiries: kingstonacs@state.gov
Visa Inquiries: kingstoniv@state.gov

The Department of State provides a list of English-speaking attorneys in Jamaica; however, it does not assume responsibility or liability for the qualifications, reputation, or quality of services provided by the listed entities or individual. The information is provided directly by the service providers, and the Department cannot verify its accuracy. To access a list of English-speaking attorneys in Jamaica, visit the Embassy's website under "U.S. Citizen Services" and select "Legal Assistance"; this will provide a list of attorneys within each consular district within Jamaica.

Additionally, foreign nationals can also apply for legal aid if they are unable to afford private legal representation. However, while the legal framework provides for these rights, practical access to legal counsel can sometimes be delayed or complicated by language barriers, limited resources, or logistical challenges, especially in cases involving foreign detainees. The Legal Aid Act in Jamaica provides for the appointment of legal aid lawyers for individuals who meet the criteria, ensuring that even those without financial means can receive defense in criminal matters, including foreigners who may be in detention.

Bail

Jamaica has a bail system that allows individuals who have been arrested to apply for release while awaiting trial, with the understanding that they are presumed innocent until proven guilty. The system is designed to balance the rights of the accused with the need for public safety and justice. Generally, most people arrested are eligible for bail, but there are exceptions, particularly for serious crimes such as murder or those involving firearms, where bail may be denied due to the risk of flight or the threat to public safety.

Bail hearings are usually held in a magistrate's court, but for more serious cases, a judge in the Supreme Court may handle the decision. During these hearings, both the defense and prosecution present arguments. The prosecution may oppose bail, citing concerns like the defendant's potential flight risk or danger to the public. While the bail system generally operates to allow for pre-trial release, the court can deny bail for those charged with particularly serious offenses or for individuals with a history of criminal behavior.

Foreign detainees are generally eligible for bail under Jamaican law, provided they meet the same criteria as Jamaican citizens. The decision to grant bail is typically based on factors like the nature of the offense, the risk of flight, ties to the community, and the potential for further criminal activity. However, there are special considerations for foreign nationals that may impact the bail process, key consideration being the risk of fleeing the country. Courts may be more cautious when granting bail to foreign nationals, especially if the accused does not have strong ties to Jamaica, such as family or a permanent residence. In such cases, the court may impose stricter conditions, like higher bail amounts or the surrender of travel documents, including passports, to prevent the individual from leaving the country before their trial.

Additionally, the court may require the foreign detainee to provide sureties, such as a local sponsor or guarantor who is a Jamaican citizen or resident, to vouch for their appearance in court. The goal is to ensure that foreign detainees, like any other defendant, will return for trial and not pose a risk to public safety or justice. However, in cases involving serious offenses, such as drug trafficking or violent crimes, the court might deny bail altogether, regardless of nationality.

Complaints Against Police

The Jamaican police force has a mixed reputation. While many officers are dedicated and professional, the force has been criticized for corruption, abuse of power, and human rights violations. Issues like bribery, excessive use of force, racial profiling, and extrajudicial killings have damaged the public's trust. Efforts have been made to improve accountability and reform, including community policing initiatives and the establishment of the Police Civilian Oversight Authority, however despite these improvements, the reputation of the Jamaican Constabulary Force remains a subject of concern, especially among vulnerable communities and foreign visitors.

To file a complaint against the police in Jamaica, individuals can report the incident to the Independent Commission of Investigations (INDECOM), which is tasked with investigating police misconduct. Complaints can be made in person at any INDECOM office, via their website (https://www.indecom.gov.jm/report-an-incident), or by calling their hotline (1-888-991-5555 or 1-888-935-5550). Additionally, individuals can contact the Public Defender's Office, which advocates for citizens' rights, including issues related to police actions. It's important to provide as much detail as possible, including names, dates, and a clear description of the incident. For serious or urgent matters, filing a report with INDECOM is the recommended route, as they have the authority to investigate and take action against police officers involved in misconduct.

Human rights organizations also play a crucial role in addressing complaints against the Jamaican police by advocating for accountability, transparency, and justice. These organizations monitor police conduct, support victims of police abuse, and raise awareness about violations of human rights. They provide a platform for individuals to report abuse, offer legal advice, and, in some cases, assist with filing complaints or seeking redress. They often work with international bodies to highlight systemic issues within law enforcement and push for reforms.

 **Human Rights Organizations in Jamaica**

Human rights organizations in Jamaica are mostly located in Kingston and Montego Bay:

- **INDEPENDENT JAMAICA COUNCIL FOR HUMAN RIGHTS**
  131 Tower Street; Kingston, Jamaica, W.I.
  Telephone: 876-967-1204
  Hours: Monday - Thursday 8:30 a.m. to 4:30 p.m.;
  Friday 8:30 a.m. to 4 p.m.
  Phone: 876-967-1204
  Email: ahh109tower@gmail.com

- **JAMAICANS FOR JUSTICE**
  2 Fagan Avenue; Kingston 8
  Website: https://dogoodjamaica.org/organization-search/item/jamaicans_for_justice/
  Email: ja.for.justice@cwjamaica.com
  Hours: Monday – Thursday 9 a.m. to 5 p.m.;

Friday 9 a.m. to 4 p.m.
Contact: Carolyn Gomes, Executive Director
Phone: 876-755-4524-6

 **General Questions**

1. *If I am convicted in Jamaica, am I likely to be released on bail pending the outcome of my appeal?* **Yes**, but the timeframe to obtain bail depends on the seriousness of the crime. If the original conviction occurred in Resident Magistrate Court, the accused will likely be released on bail during the appeal. If the original conviction occurred in the Supreme Court, the criminal conviction is more serious and will likely be denied during the appeal process.

2. *What influences a bail determination?* In Jamaica, bail determinations are influenced by several key factors, including the severity of the offense, the likelihood of the defendant appearing for trial, and whether the defendant poses a threat to public safety or witnesses. Judges consider the strength of the evidence, the defendant's criminal history, and the risk of reoffending. The court also looks at the potential for the defendant to interfere with the investigation or the judicial process.

3. *Who is entitled to bail?* Under the Bail Act of 2000, most individuals charged with a crime are entitled to apply for bail, though it may be denied for serious offenses like murder or drug trafficking, or if the court deems the person a flight risk or a danger to public safety. Factors like prior convictions or a history of skipping court may also affect bail decisions.

4. ***If I am arrested, how soon will I see a judge or magistrate?*** If you're arrested, you must be brought before a judge or magistrate within 24- 48 hours, as required by law. This is to ensure that your detention is reviewed, and that you are informed of the charges against you. If you're not brought to court within this time frame, your detention may be considered unlawful, and you could be entitled to release. The first appearance typically involves a bail hearing or a decision on whether the case will proceed.

5. ***Will I be able to contact my country's embassy in Jamaica?*** If you're arrested in Jamaica, you have the right to contact your country's embassy or consulate. Under international law, foreign nationals are entitled to consular assistance when detained. You should notify the police of your desire to contact your embassy, and they are required to facilitate this request.

JAILS VS. PRISONS: CONDITIONS & CULTURE

JAILS VS. PRISONS: CONDITIONS & CULTURE

Overview

The primary purpose of jails and prisons in Jamaica is to detain individuals who have been accused or convicted of criminal offenses, with the goal of rehabilitating offenders, protecting society, and enforcing justice. Both institutions serve as places of incarceration, but there are key differences between them, largely revolving around the length of incarceration and the security measures in place,

Jails in Jamaica are typically used for short-term detention. They house individuals who are awaiting trial or sentencing, or those who have been sentenced to short-term imprisonment (usually less than one year). Jails are more often associated with pre-trial detainees and those convicted of less severe offenses. **Prisons,** on the other hand, are designed for long-term incarceration. They house individuals convicted of serious crimes and sentenced to extended terms of imprisonment, often for years or life. Prisons in Jamaica are equipped with more stringent security measures and typically offer programs aimed at rehabilitation and reintegration into society for long-term offenders.

Jamaica's jails and prisons operate under the management of the Department of Correctional Services (DCS), which is part of the Ministry of National Security. The largest and most prominent correctional facility in Jamaica, is **Tower Street Adult Correctional Centre** (aka "Kingston Adult Prison") in Kingston, which houses a significant portion of the country's male inmates and is designed for long-term incarceration. Another major prison, located in the parish of St. Catherine, **St. Catherine Adult Correctional Centre**, houses both male and female prisoners, including those sentenced for serious offenses. **The Correctional Centre at Tamarind Farm**, also St. Catherine, however is intended specifically for female inmates.

Prisons and correctional centers in Jamaica operate under strict security protocols. This includes perimeter fences, surveillance, and controlled access to and from the facilities. Some prisons have different levels of security based on the severity of the inmates' offenses.

The Jamaican prison population is primarily made up of male inmates convicted for crimes like murder, robbery, drug offenses, and sexual assault. A smaller percentage consists of foreign nationals from regions such as North America and the Caribbean. Many individuals are also held on remand, awaiting trial or sentencing. While the system is criticized for overcrowding and a focus on punishment over rehabilitation, efforts are being made to address the needs of certain groups, such as those incarcerated for minor offenses or with mental health issues.

Prison Conditions and Living Environment

Jamaican prisons and jails classify inmates based on security levels, which include maximum, medium, and minimum security, with each level corresponding to the severity of the offenses committed and the risks posed by the inmates. Maximum-security facilities house high-risk offenders, including violent criminals, with strict security measures to prevent escapes and maintain control. Medium-security units are for offenders who are less dangerous but still pose some risk, while minimum-security facilities accommodate non-violent offenders or those with good behavior, often offering more privileges and opportunities for rehabilitation.

Men and women are generally separated in jails and prisons. Male and female prisoners are housed in distinct facilities or separate wings within the same facility to ensure security and to adhere to human rights standards. This separation is in place to protect both genders from potential harm and to meet the legal requirements for housing inmates. However, the conditions and resources available in female facilities have been reported as less adequate compared to those for male prisoners, which is a concern for human rights advocates.

Jamaican jails and prisons are generally reported to be overcrowded and inadequate, which often leads to a strain on resources and basic facilities. Inmates frequently face unsanitary conditions, with limited access to clean water, poor ventilation, and inadequate bedding. While inmates receive basic meals, their nutritional quality and preparation are often subpar, and many prisoners rely on family support for additional food. Overcrowding exacerbates the challenges of maintaining hygiene, providing medical care, and ensuring overall safety. This overcrowding also makes it difficult for correctional staff to manage and supervise inmates effectively, sometimes leading to violent incidents and unrest within the facilities. While there are some efforts at rehabilitation and vocational training, these are often limited by the lack of resources, and prisoners may not receive the necessary support to reintegrate successfully into society.

Medical care within Jamaican prisons is another area of concern, with reports suggesting that inmates have limited access to health services, particularly for chronic conditions and mental health issues. Despite the implementation of programs aimed at education and rehabilitation, these initiatives are not always accessible to all inmates due to resource constraints. In addition, many inmates experience delays in legal processes, contributing to lengthy periods of detention before trial.

Inmate Rights and Legal Protections[10]

In Jamaica, prisoners retain certain constitutional rights despite their incarceration, although these rights can be limited by the nature of

---

10 https://mlca.gov.jm/
    fundamental-rights-of-citizens-guaranteed-in-jamaicas-constitution/

imprisonment. The Constitution of Jamaica guarantees the protection of fundamental human rights, which extend to those who are incarcerated, subject to lawful restrictions.

Some key constitutional rights of prisoners in Jamaica include:

- **Right to Fair Treatment and Dignity:** Under the Constitution, all persons are entitled to be treated with dignity and respect. This means that prisoners should not be subjected to inhuman or degrading treatment. However, the reality of prison conditions often falls short of this ideal due to overcrowding and inadequate facilities.

- **Right to Legal Representation:** Prisoners have the right to legal counsel, and they can contact a lawyer or request legal assistance. This is crucial for ensuring access to justice and fair trial, particularly for those who cannot afford private legal representation. The legal aid system provides support to indigent prisoners.

- **Right to be Free from Arbitrary Detention:** The Constitution guarantees protection from arbitrary detention, meaning that prisoners should not be held without lawful cause. This includes the right to be brought before a court within a reasonable time (usually 48 hours) after arrest.

- **Right to Access to the Courts:** Prisoners retain the right to challenge their detention and any conditions of their imprisonment in court. They can file complaints, request bail hearings, and seek redress for any violation of their rights through legal channels.

- **Right to Health Care:** The Jamaican Constitution does not explicitly guarantee prisoners' access to healthcare, but they do have the right to basic medical treatment. The government is responsible for providing health services to inmates, although this is often limited due to resource constraints.

- **Right to Communicate:** Prisoners have the right to communicate with the outside world, including their family, legal representatives, and consular officials, although these communications may be monitored or restricted for security reasons.

- **Freedom from Slavery and Forced Labor:** While prisoners may be required to work, they cannot be subjected to forced or exploitative labor, as this would violate constitutional protections against slavery and servitude.

In Jamaica, foreign detainees are entitled to the same legal rights as Jamaican citizens, including the right to legal representation. They can request to contact an attorney of their choice, and if they cannot afford one, they may apply for legal aid. In addition to this, foreign detainees have the right to consular assistance from their embassy or consulate, which can help them secure legal counsel and provide support throughout their case. They are also allowed to communicate with their legal representative and consular officials, ensuring they are fully informed and their rights are protected.

 **General Questions**

1. *What is the difference between a jail and prison in Jamaica?*
   The main difference between jail and prison lies in their function and the length of stay. Jails are typically for individuals awaiting trial or serving short sentences, while prisons are for those convicted of more serious crimes and serving longer sentences. Prisons have more secure facilities and are designed for long-term incarceration, whereas jails are more temporary holding centers.

2. *Do jails and prisons offer religious services to inmates?* In Jamaica, most jails and prisons offer religious programs to inmates. These programs are typically facilitated by chaplains or religious organizations and include services, counseling, and spiritual support. They aim to provide inmates with opportunities for personal reflection, moral guidance, and rehabilitation through faith-based initiatives. The programs are part of efforts to support the rehabilitation process and help individuals reintegrate into society upon release.

3. *How do prisoners spend their time?* In Jamaican prisons, inmates follow a structured daily routine, which includes work assignments, educational programs, and rehabilitation activities. They may engage in tasks like cleaning, kitchen duties, or vocational training. Some facilities offer religious programs and counseling sessions, while physical exercise and recreation help maintain health. Inmates also have scheduled visitation times for family and legal representatives. The day typically ends with a headcount and confinement to cells for the night, with the focus on maintaining order while providing opportunities for personal growth and rehabilitation.

4. *What type of jobs can inmates perform?* In Jamaican prisons, inmates are often assigned various jobs aimed at keeping the facility running efficiently and providing them with skills for reintegration into society. Common jobs include kitchen duties, where prisoners help prepare meals; cleaning tasks, such as maintaining the prison grounds and facilities; and laundry services. Some prisoners are also involved in vocational training, which may include carpentry, farming, or garment-making. These jobs serve both to contribute to the prison's operation and offer inmates opportunities to acquire practical skills that may help them upon release.

5. *How does the prison commissary system work in Jamaica?* In Jamaican prisons, the commissary system allows inmates to buy personal items like hygiene products, snacks, and phone cards using money deposited into their accounts by family or friends. The prices are typically higher than outside, and the goods available are limited. While this system provides some autonomy, it can create disparities, as prisoners without financial support may have less access to these extra amenities.

6. ***What type of medical care do prisoners receive?*** In Jamaican prisons, medical care is provided, but the quality and availability can be limited due to resource constraints. Each facility has a basic infirmary where inmates can receive treatment for minor ailments and injuries. However, for more serious conditions, prisoners may be transferred to public hospitals or specialized clinics. Access to healthcare can be slow, and there are concerns about overcrowding, insufficient medical staff, and delays in treatment, especially for mental health services.

7. ***What is prison culture in Jamaica?*** Prison culture is shaped by strict hierarchies, gang influence, and a focus on survival. Inmates often form alliances based on shared backgrounds or offenses, with violence being a common way to maintain respect or power. While some engage in rehabilitation programs, the pervasive culture of toughness and group dynamics can overshadow efforts for personal growth. Despite the harsh environment, religious practices and small support networks provide a sense of community for many prisoners.

HELPING A FRIEND OR RELATIVE IMPRISONED IN JAMAICA

CHAPTER 12
HELPING A FRIEND OR RELATIVE IMPRISONED IN JAMAICA

Overview

If your loved one is arrested and imprisoned in Jamaica, it's important to take immediate action to ensure their safety and secure legal representation. The first step is to contact the police station where they are being held to inquire about their condition, the charges they face, and any potential bail options. Understanding the charges and whether they are eligible for bail is crucial at this stage.

Next, reach out to the U.S. Embassy in Kingston (or your respective embassy if you're from another country) for assistance. The embassy can provide vital consular support. Embassy staff can help by notifying family members of the arrest, ensuring the detainee's rights are respected, and providing a list of English-speaking attorneys. Although the embassy cannot directly intervene in the legal process, they can make sure the individual has access to legal representation and that the conditions of their detention meet international human rights standards.

It's critical to hire an experienced English-speaking lawyer to represent your loved one in Jamaica's legal system. You can ask the embassy for a list of recommended attorneys, or you can directly contact law firms that specialize in criminal defense. Your lawyer will be able to help navigate the bail process, negotiate terms, and prepare a defense.

In addition, it's important to inquire about the detainee's health and well-being. You can send care packages or money, if necessary, as prison conditions may be harsh, and resources limited. Ensure your loved one receives adequate food, medical care, and hygiene supplies. The Jamaican prison system may not always provide these basic needs, and family members often need to step in to ensure proper care.

Throughout the process, document every interaction you have with the police, embassy, and lawyer. Having a detailed record will help you stay organized and informed. Stay in touch with local authorities and the embassy to keep up with any developments in the case.

Finally, be aware that the Jamaican legal system may differ from what you're accustomed to. While your loved one is entitled to legal representation, the process can be lengthy and sometimes challenging, especially when dealing with foreign nationals. The key is to remain calm, stay informed, and work closely with legal professionals to secure the best possible outcome for your loved one.

 For information related to helping a loved one jailed in Jamaica, visit **https://jm.usembassy.gov/u-s-citizen-services/arrest-of-a-u-s-citizen**

Sending Supplies and Money to an Inmate

In Jamaica, prisons may have specific rules on what supplies you can send to an inmate. These could include food, toiletries, clothing, or other personal items. It's crucial to check with the specific facility where your loved one is held to confirm what can be sent and how. Some prisons have restrictions on items like cigarettes, alcohol, or electronic devices.

You can usually send a care package with basic necessities such as toiletries (soap, toothpaste, etc.), hygiene products, and non-perishable food items. In some cases, these items need to be sent through approved channels or at specific times. Check with the prison administration to confirm how these packages should be delivered.

Food packages are sometimes allowed, but these too must meet certain standards. Most facilities require that food be non-perishable and packaged in a way that can be easily inspected. Processed and packaged food like canned goods or sealed snack items are generally allowed, but homemade items or perishable goods might not be.

Prisons may have rules about the types of clothing or personal items inmates can have. For example, certain colors or styles may be prohibited, and items like blankets or shoes might need to be purchased from a commissary instead of sent from the outside.

Additionally, some prisons may have partnerships with local vendors, meaning you can order and send supplies through specific channels. In some cases, a third-party service may handle the delivery, which can ensure that the items meet the prison's guidelines.

To send money to a loved one in a Jamaican prison from the USA, you typically use money transfer services. The two most commonly used options are:

- **Western Union:** You can send money via Western Union either online (through their website or mobile app) or by visiting a local Western Union agent location. Payments can be made using a bank account, credit/debit card, or cash, depending on the method you choose.
- **MoneyGram:** Similar to Western Union, you can use MoneyGram to send funds online, through their website or app, or at a physical MoneyGram location. The funds are typically deposited into the recipient's prison account.

You will need the inmate's prison number and full name to ensure the money is deposited into the correct account. It's also important to double-check with the prison for any specific instructions or restrictions regarding how the money should be sent (some prisons may require additional information or specific forms). Both Western Union and MoneyGram charge fees for transferring money, and the amount you can send may be subject to limits. Fees vary depending on the amount being sent, the method of transfer, and the destination. Some Jamaican prisons may also accept money orders or bank transfers, though these options can be more complicated and may require you to work directly with the facility.

If you're unsure of the rules and procedures, a lawyer familiar with the Jamaican legal system can provide guidance. They can also communicate with the prison on your behalf to ensure that your loved one receives the necessary supplies in a timely manner. Laws and policies regarding inmate welfare can change, so it's always important to stay updated on any new regulations that might affect the sending of money or supplies.

Mail and Visitation

Sending mail to an inmate requires attention to detail. Each facility in Jamaica has its own mailing address, and it's crucial that you include the correct details, such as the inmate's full name and ID number. When sending mail, avoid prohibited items such as cash, weapons, or explicit content. Letters, books, and magazines are generally allowed but must come from publishers or legitimate sources. Postage is standard, and while the mail is usually inspected for security purposes, it's important to ensure no contraband is included, as this could result in the rejection of the mail.

For visiting an inmate, it's necessary to follow the prison's visiting hours and ensure you are on the approved visitors list. Visitors must present valid ID, and there are strict regulations on dress code and behavior within the facility. You can expect a thorough security screening, including bag checks and metal detectors, to prevent contraband from entering. Physical contact with inmates is typically restricted, and you may be required to speak through a glass partition or with a guard present. Visits are often brief and monitored. However, some prisons are beginning to offer video calls as an alternative, especially during times of heightened health concerns.

Prison Scams

Like in many countries, there are several common prison scams in Jamaica that both inmates and their families need to be aware of to avoid being exploited. These scams typically involve fraudulent schemes designed to trick individuals into sending money, goods, or providing help under false pretenses. One common scam involves inmates or individuals pretending to be prisoners, asking family members for money to cover legal fees, bribes, or emergencies. These requests may be for things like food or medical supplies, but they can often be false. Another scam involves fraudulent legal assistance, where individuals posing as lawyers offer help for a fee but never deliver.

In some cases, inmates may try to involve family members in smuggling contraband, like cell phones or drugs, by sending items through mail, which is illegal. There are also scams where prisoners claim to have influence within the system, promising special treatment or protection for a price. Lastly, inmates might overcharge for commissary items or have their families buy unnecessary goods. To avoid falling victim, families should always verify requests through official channels, like the prison authorities or trusted legal advisors, before sending money or supplies.

Upon Release

When an American citizen is released from a Jamaican prison, there are several critical steps and stipulations they must consider before returning to the United States. First, if the individual has been convicted of a serious crime, Jamaican authorities may initiate deportation proceedings once they have served their sentence. U.S. citizens convicted abroad, particularly for felonies, often face automatic deportation. This means that once their sentence is completed, they may be required to leave Jamaica and return to the U.S., depending on their criminal history.

Upon release, the individual can seek assistance from the U.S. Embassy in Kingston. The embassy can help with passport services, provide legal advice, and assist in ensuring the person has the necessary documentation to return home. In some cases, if deportation is necessary, Jamaican authorities may facilitate travel arrangements and issue the necessary travel documents. However, if the individual is arranging their own travel, the embassy can also provide guidance, although they will need to cover the cost themselves.

Once they return to the U.S., the individual could face complications depending on the nature of their conviction. A criminal record abroad, particularly for serious offenses, may make reentry difficult. The person could be detained by U.S. Customs and Border Protection (CBP) and subjected to additional immigration hearings or even denied entry. If reentry is granted, the individual may also be placed under post-release supervision, such as probation or monitoring by U.S. Immigration and Customs Enforcement (ICE), depending on the severity of their crime.

Before traveling, it is crucial for any American citizen released from a Jamaican prison to consult with the U.S. Embassy and legal professionals to ensure they understand their rights, immigration implications, and any legal hurdles they may face when returning to the U.S.

THE ADMINISTRATION OF JUSTICE

THE ADMINISTRATION OF JUSTICE

Jamaica's Legal System

Jamaica's legal system is based on the English common law tradition, a heritage from the country's colonial past under British rule. This system is characterized by the reliance on case law (judicial precedents) and statutes passed by the Jamaican Parliament. The judiciary in Jamaica is independent, meaning that it operates separately from the executive and legislative branches of government, ensuring impartiality in the interpretation and application of the law.

The legal system is primarily focused on upholding justice, ensuring that laws are fairly applied, and protecting the rights of individuals. Courts in Jamaica play a central role in resolving disputes, whether they are criminal, civil, or family-related. The system emphasizes the protection of human rights, as enshrined in the Jamaican Constitution, and provides avenues for individuals to challenge government actions or seek legal remedies for violations of their rights.

Jamaica also has a robust legal framework for criminal justice, aiming to maintain law and order while balancing the protection of individual freedoms. Laws are made by the Parliament, and they apply equally to all citizens, though the judiciary has the responsibility to interpret and apply them according to the circumstances of each case. Legal professionals, including judges, attorneys, and legal advisors, uphold the integrity of the system by providing legal representation, ensuring that both the accused and the victims receive fair treatment throughout legal proceedings.

While the system is largely grounded in British legal traditions, Jamaica has developed its own set of legal norms and principles, reflecting the country's unique cultural, social, and political context. Over time, the Jamaican legal system has made adjustments to address local issues, particularly in areas like human rights, equality, and social justice.

The Judiciary[11]

Jamaica's judiciary is structured into several levels of courts, each with distinct responsibilities and functions. The judicial system is designed to handle various types of cases, from minor offenses to serious constitutional issues, with each court having its defined jurisdiction and role.

1. **The Court of Appeal:** This is the highest court in Jamaica and primarily hears appeals from the Supreme Court, the Resident Magistrate's Courts, and other lower courts. The Court of Appeal's responsibilities include reviewing legal decisions, interpreting laws, and ensuring justice is served by correcting errors made in lower courts. Its judgments can set important precedents that influence future legal cases.

2. **The Supreme Court:** The Supreme Court is the second highest level in Jamaica's judicial hierarchy and handles more serious criminal and civil cases. It has both original and appellate jurisdiction, meaning it can hear cases for the first time or hear appeals from lower courts. The Supreme Court also deals with constitutional matters, judicial reviews, and actions against public bodies. Cases that involve constitutional issues, human rights, or significant public interest are often addressed here.

3. **The Parish Courts:** These are the courts of first instance for most minor criminal and civil matters. They handle less severe criminal

---

11   https://jis.gov.jm/government/the-judiciary

cases, such as theft, assault, and drug possession, as well as civil cases involving smaller sums of money. Parish Courts also deal with family law matters, including child custody and maintenance, and have special jurisdictions in areas like the Small Claims Court.

4. **Family Court:** The Family Court deals specifically with cases related to family law, including child abuse, domestic violence, divorce, child custody, and child support. The court aims to provide quick, accessible, and fair resolutions for issues that affect the well-being of families, especially children.

5. **Magistrate's Court:** This court deals with minor offenses and preliminary hearings for serious criminal offenses. It handles cases like petty theft, traffic violations, and breaches of the peace. It can also issue warrants, oversee bail applications, and conduct preliminary hearings for serious cases before they are sent to the Supreme Court.

The primary responsibilities of Jamaica's courts include ensuring justice, interpreting the law, and upholding the Constitution. They are tasked with resolving disputes, administering criminal justice, and safeguarding citizens' rights by ensuring that laws are fairly and impartially applied. In addition, courts are responsible for setting legal precedents that guide future cases, overseeing legal procedures, and protecting the rights of all individuals, including marginalized groups. The judiciary's independence is vital in maintaining the rule of law and ensuring that all parties have access to fair trials and justice.

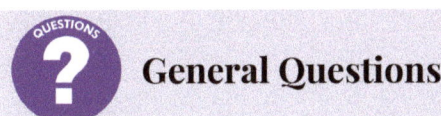

General Questions

1. *Will the court treat first-time offenders and tourists with more leniency?* In Jamaica, first-time offenders and tourists are not automatically granted leniency, but certain factors may influence sentencing. First-time offenders may receive more lenient treatment, especially if they show remorse or have a clean record, with options like probation or community service being considered

for less severe crimes. For tourists, the court may take into account their visitor status, particularly for less serious offenses, but serious crimes are prosecuted equally regardless of nationality. Ultimately, while the Jamaican legal system ensures equality before the law, judges may consider personal circumstances when determining appropriate sentences.

2. *If I am charged with a crime, which court is likely to hear my case?* In Jamaica, the court that will hear your case depends on the severity of the charge. Less serious offenses, like minor theft or assault, are typically handled in the Magistrate's Court, where the penalties are less severe. However, more serious crimes such as murder, rape, or large-scale drug offenses are tried in the High Court, which has the authority to impose harsher penalties, including long prison sentences. The initial determination of which court hears the case often depends on the nature of the crime and can involve referral from one court to another for more complex matters.

3. *What is the standard of proof in a criminal case in Jamaica?* Like in the U.S., the standard of proof in a criminal case in Jamaica is "beyond a reasonable doubt." This is the highest standard of proof used in the legal system and means that the prosecution must present evidence that leaves the court with no reasonable doubt about the defendant's guilt. If the evidence does not meet this standard, the accused must be acquitted.

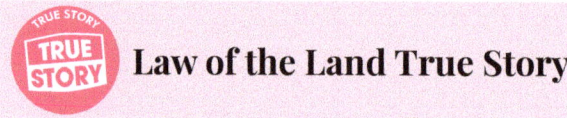

Law of the Land True Story

A 36-year-old male teacher at a prominent high school in Westmoreland in Jamaica, who was arrested and charged for allegedly raping a 16-year-old female student of the institution, was granted bail in the sum of $500,000 with surety when he appeared in the Westmoreland Parish Court on Tuesday, June 25, 2019.

The accused, Jerome Heron, was booked and ordered to return to court on July 24. He was ordered to surrender his travel documents and to report to the Savanna-la-Mar Police Station on Mondays, Wednesdays and Saturdays as conditions of his bail. He was also banned from working anywhere around girls of 16 or less years old. According to police reports, the offense was committed at the school on Friday, February 1, 2019. The Westmoreland police said further investigations are being conducted into other sexual-related offenses that have reportedly been committed against other female students at the same educational institution.

Takeaways

- Jamaica's legal system is based on the English common law tradition, with an emphasis on case law (judicial precedents) and statutory law passed by Parliament. The judiciary is independent, ensuring impartial application of the law.

- Jamaica's judiciary includes several levels of courts:

  - The Court of Appeal is the highest court, mainly handling appeals.

  - The Supreme Court hears serious criminal and civil cases, including constitutional matters.

  - The Parish Courts deal with minor criminal and civil matters.

  - The Family Court handles family law issues like child custody and domestic violence.

  - The Magistrate's Court oversees minor offenses and preliminary hearings for more serious cases.

  - The Jamaican legal system emphasizes the protection of human rights and provides avenues for individuals to challenge violations. Courts play a key role in interpreting the law, ensuring fairness, and maintaining the rule of law.

- While first-time offenders and tourists are not automatically granted leniency, factors such as remorse or the nature of the offense may influence sentencing. Serious crimes are treated equally, regardless of nationality. The severity of the crime typically determines which court hears the case.

CRIME VICTIM ASSISTANCE

CRIME VICTIM ASSISTANCE

Overview

 While police assistance is available throughout Jamaica, the level of support offered to foreign crime victims can differ, ranging from partial to full involvement. This variation is mainly due to challenges such as a lack of personnel, inadequate training, limited vehicle availability, and overall resource constraints within the police force.

As a foreign visitor to Jamaica, you have access to various crime victim assistance services, including support from both government agencies and non-governmental organizations (NGOs). The **Jamaica Constabulary Force (JCF)** and the **Victim Support Unit (VSU)** offer immediate help, including crisis counseling, victim advocacy, and assistance navigating the criminal justice system. You can report a crime by contacting the police directly or using the **Crime Stop Hotline** at **311**. Additionally, the **Legal Aid Council** provides free legal representation for those unable to afford a lawyer.

For more specialized support, organizations like the **Rape Crisis Centre** and the **Women's Resource and Outreach Centre (WROC)** assist victims of sexual assault and domestic violence, offering counseling, legal advice, and shelter. If you need medical attention after a crime, you can visit any hospital or clinic in Jamaica. The **Jamaican Red Cross** also provides first aid and emergency relief services.

As a foreigner, you can also seek assistance from your **embassy or consulate**, which can help coordinate emergency travel, legal referrals, and liaise with local authorities. In some cases, you may be eligible for compensation or restitution through the **National Crime Prevention Fund** or other legal channels. These resources ensure that you receive the necessary support, whether it's legal, emotional, or practical, during your recovery after a crime.

What to Do if You Are the Victim of a Crime

If you find yourself a victim of crime while visiting Jamaica, the situation can feel overwhelming, but it's important to stay calm and take the necessary steps to ensure your safety and access the support you need.

The first thing you should do is make sure you're safe. If you're in immediate danger, try to move to a secure location, whether that's a nearby hotel, a public area, or any place where you can find assistance or protection. Once you're out of harm's way, assess your physical well-being. If you've been injured, seek medical attention right away. You can go to any nearby hospital or clinic, or if needed, dial **911** for emergency services. The **Jamaican Red Cross** can also provide immediate first aid if necessary.

Next, it's essential to report the crime to local authorities. The **Jamaica Constabulary Force** (**JCF**) is the official law enforcement agency in Jamaica, and you can reach them by calling **119** (the emergency number), or by visiting the nearest police station. If you need help with directions or feel unsafe traveling on your own, your hotel or resort staff can assist in contacting the police. Once at the police station, you'll be asked to provide a detailed account of what happened, so be prepared to describe the crime, the location, and any details you remember about the incident. If there were witnesses, mention them as well.

After reporting the crime, you should reach out to the **Victim Support Unit** (**VSU**), which is part of the Jamaican police force. The VSU provides critical services, including emotional support, counseling, and guidance through the legal process. They can also help connect you to other services, such as legal aid or shelters, depending on your needs. You can contact them directly at **1-888-991-4000** or ask local authorities for their assistance. If you're facing legal difficulties or need legal advice, the **Legal Aid Council** offers free legal services for those who cannot afford a lawyer. Additionally, your embassy or consulate can provide invaluable assistance, from helping you liaise with local authorities to offering guidance on legal matters. They can even help you contact an attorney or arrange for emergency travel if necessary.

As you recover from the ordeal, it's important to document everything related to the crime. Keep copies of the police report, medical records, any photos or evidence you may have, and notes on all interactions with law enforcement and victim support services. This documentation will be helpful if you need to file an insurance claim, pursue legal action, or simply keep track of the case's progress.

Finally, follow up with local authorities and victim support services regularly. Investigations can take time, but staying engaged will help ensure you receive the assistance you need. Whether it's checking on the status of your case, accessing ongoing counseling, or understanding your legal options, staying in touch with the right organizations will help you navigate through the process with more clarity and support.

Common Tourist Scams in Jamaica

While Jamaica is a beautiful and welcoming destination for travelers, like many popular tourist spots, it is not immune to financial scams targeting foreign visitors. Criminals often exploit tourists who may be unfamiliar with local practices, currency, or common scams. Here are some of the most common financial scams that foreign visitors to Jamaica should be aware of:

- **Fake Taxi Scams:** Unscrupulous individuals pose as legitimate taxi drivers, offering rides at inflated prices or taking tourists to isolated locations. Always use licensed taxis and agree on a price before getting in.

- **Currency Exchange Scams:** Scammers offer to exchange money at attractive rates but provide counterfeit bills or charge hidden fees. Stick to reputable exchange offices, banks, or official hotel services.

- **Overcharging at Shops and Restaurants:** Tourists are often charged more than locals for goods and services, particularly in tourist-heavy areas. Always confirm prices beforehand and check your bill carefully.

- **Timeshare or Vacation Package Scams:** Fraudsters offer "too-good-to-be-true" deals on timeshares or vacation packages, pressuring visitors into signing contracts. Research thoroughly and avoid high-pressure sales tactics.

- **Street Vendor Overcharging:** In popular tourist areas, vendors may inflate prices when dealing with tourists. Negotiate prices or compare rates to ensure you're not being overcharged.

To protect yourself, the first step is to do your research before you travel. Familiarizing yourself with common scams can help you spot red flags when they arise. Ask your hotel or locals about typical prices for goods and services in the area to avoid being overcharged. Trust your instincts—if something feels too good to be true or makes you uncomfortable, walk away. Always use trusted services, whether it's booking taxis, tours, or exchanging currency. Stick to licensed taxis, official exchange offices, and established travel agencies to minimize risk.

Another key precaution is to be mindful of where and how you share your personal information. Avoid giving out your credit card details to unsolicited sources and never make transactions on unsecured Wi-Fi networks. Use common sense: If a vendor is aggressive or pressures you into a quick decision, it's often a sign to back off. Lastly, if anything feels suspicious—whether it's an offer that's too good to be true or a high-pressure sales tactic—remember, it's okay to say no and walk away.

Sexual Assault

If you are a victim of sexual assault in Jamaica, it's important to understand the steps you can take to seek help, report the incident, and start your healing journey. The first priority is ensuring your immediate safety. If possible, get to a safe place—a friend's home, a public area, or even a police station. Once you are safe, seek medical attention right away. Even if you don't feel injured, it's essential to have a medical professional examine you, as they can help treat any physical injuries, prevent the transmission of sexually transmitted infections (STIs), and preserve evidence of the assault.

In Jamaica, healthcare facilities can perform a forensic examination, to collect vital evidence. This examination should ideally be done within 72 hours of the assault. The Ministry of Health and Wellness provides free medical care to sexual assault survivors, including treatment for STIs, emergency contraception, and other necessary care.

Once you've sought medical attention, the next step is to report the assault to the police. You can do this by calling the emergency number **119** or going to the nearest police station. In Jamaica, specialized units like the **Centre for the Investigation of Sexual Offences and Child Abuse (CISOCA)** are trained to handle these sensitive cases with care and respect. The Sexual Offences Act of 2017 ensures that sexual assault is treated as a serious criminal offense, and as a victim, you have the right to pursue justice.

It's important to know your rights throughout this process. You have the right to privacy, meaning your identity and personal information will be protected. You also have the right to legal assistance. If you cannot afford a lawyer, you can access legal aid through the **Legal Aid Council** or seek help from private attorneys. If you fear for your safety, you can request protective measures, such as a restraining order, through the police or courts.

Healing from sexual assault is a deeply personal experience, and accessing psychosocial support is critical. In Jamaica, organizations like the **Jamaica Red Cross**, the **Women's Centre of Jamaica Foundation**, and the **Rape Crisis Society** offer counseling and emotional support. Surrounding yourself with family, friends, and support groups can also help you process the emotional and psychological impact of the assault.

In addition to counseling, several non-governmental organizations (NGOs) such as **Jamaica Advocacy for Sexual Assault Victims (JASAV)**, The **Women's Resource and Outreach Centre (WROC)**, and the **Jamaica Network of Seropositives (JN+)** provide advocacy, legal support, and community resources for survivors.

If you decide to move forward with legal action, the police will investigate, gathering evidence and interviewing witnesses. As the case progresses, you have the right to be informed about its status. If the case goes to court, you may be required to testify, but the legal system in Jamaica allows for victim support, such as the option to give testimony via video or behind a screen to minimize trauma.

Throughout this process, self-care and healing should remain a priority. Take time for yourself, whether that means joining support groups for survivors or simply resting and reflecting. Everyone's journey to healing is unique, but know that resources and support are available, and you don't have to go through this alone.

Important Contacts in Jamaica

- **Jamaican Police Force:** 119 (emergency) or the nearest police station
- **CISOCA (Centre for the Investigation of Sexual Offences and Child Abuse):** (876) 926-4079 or (876) 926-3798
- **Women's Centre of Jamaica Foundation:** (876) 929-7438
- **Jamaica Red Cross:** (876) 926-2355
- **National Helpline for Domestic Violence:** (876) 922-0712 or (876) 927-1656

Consular Assistance

If you are a victim of a crime, such as sexual assault, in Jamaica, your embassy or consulate can provide essential support. While they can't intervene directly in legal matters, they can guide you through the next steps and connect you with local resources. They can help you contact the Jamaican Police Force or CISOCA and direct you to medical facilities for treatment and forensic exams to collect evidence.

The embassy can also assist with practical needs, such as issuing emergency travel documents if your passport is lost or stolen, and help you contact family for support. If the legal process feels overwhelming, they can act as a liaison with local authorities to ensure your case is handled properly.

Additionally, they can connect you to counseling services for emotional support and guide you through repatriation if you wish to leave Jamaica. While they can't provide financial aid directly, they can help you access emergency funds from family.

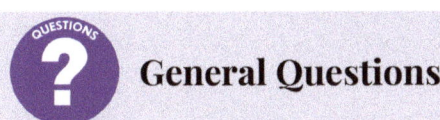

General Questions

1. *If I am a victim of a crime, can I legally be compensated?* In Jamaica, there is a Victim Compensation Fund managed by the Ministry of Justice. However, this fund primarily applies to victims of violent crimes, including sexual assault, homicide, and other forms of violent injury. To be eligible for compensation, the crime must be reported to the police, and there are often conditions attached, such as the severity of the injury or the financial need of the victim or their family. The compensation process can be complex and requires the victim (or their representative) to apply through the Ministry of Justice.

2. *If a family member falls victim to homicide, can I bring the body back to my home country?* If a family member falls victim to homicide in Jamaica, it is possible to repatriate the body to your home country, but several steps are required. First, you'll need to obtain a death certificate and, if the cause of death is under investigation, an autopsy report. A local funeral home will handle embalming and the necessary paperwork, including an embalming certificate. The body can then be transported through an airline that specializes in human remains, with proper documentation for both Jamaica and your home country. Your embassy or consulate can assist with the process, ensuring all required legal and customs procedures are followed.

3. *If a family member falls victim to homicide, will I receive any assistance from the Jamaican government?* If a family member falls victim to homicide in Jamaica, the government provides some assistance. The Jamaican Police Force, including CISOCA, will investigate the case, and the Victim Services Division offers emotional support and guidance. While the government doesn't typically cover funeral costs, they can assist with necessary documentation like death certificates. The Victim Compensation Fund may offer some support, but it mainly applies to those physically harmed by violent crime, not homicide victims. Additional help can be provided by NGOs and your embassy.

POLICE

CHAPTER 15

POLICE

Overview[12]

The **Jamaica Constabulary Force** (**JCF**), the official police body of the country, comprises approximately 10,000 members, including officers across various ranks and specialized units. These units include branches such as the Counterterrorism and Organized Crime Investigative Branch (C-TOC), the Specialized Operations Branch, and the Community Safety and Security Branch, each tasked with handling specific law enforcement challenges. Given Jamaica's population of about 2.9 million, the JCF operates with a ratio of roughly one officer for every 290 residents.

However, the force faces significant hurdles. Limited resources and budget constraints have long impacted the JCF's ability to effectively address crime, despite its relatively large personnel size. With one of the highest crime rates in the Caribbean, the JCF is under constant pressure to manage public safety and maintain order, especially in urban areas and regions affected by gang violence and organized crime. These challenges, combined with issues such as understaffing, inadequate training, and a strained relationship with some communities, highlight the complexities the force faces in its mission to serve and protect.

---

12   https://www.mns.gov.jm/node/52

Police Response

The Jamaican Constabulary Force (JCF) plays a crucial role in maintaining law and order in Jamaica through a variety of key functions. These include crime prevention, law enforcement, and public order maintenance, where officers patrol communities, investigate crimes, and enforce the law. The JCF also handles criminal investigations, with specialized units like the Criminal Investigation Branch (CIB) and C-TOC focusing on serious offenses and organized crime. They are responsible for traffic control, ensuring road safety, and managing accidents. The force also emphasizes community policing, working closely with citizens to foster trust and address local concerns. Other key duties include raising public awareness on safety, protecting vulnerable groups through units like CISOCA, and collaborating with the Jamaica Defense Force to safeguard national security. Despite its critical role, the JCF faces challenges such as limited resources and strained community relations, which complicate its efforts.

The Jamaica Constabulary Force (JCF) faces several major challenges that impact its effectiveness. Understaffing and limited resources strain the force, making it difficult to manage the high levels of crime and violence, including gang activity and organized crime. Corruption within the force further erodes public trust, as many Jamaicans perceive the police as ineffective or compromised. Additionally, the bureaucratic inefficiencies in crime reporting and investigations slow down response times and case resolutions, discouraging people from coming forward. The JCF also struggles with providing adequate training for officers, especially in specialized areas, and dealing with political influence that can undermine its operations. Furthermore, violence against police officers, particularly in high-risk areas, adds another layer of danger to their work. These systemic challenges hinder the JCF's ability to effectively serve and protect the Jamaican public.

Ongoing reforms within the Jamaica Constabulary Force (JCF) focus on modernization, community policing, and professional development. The force is upgrading technology and training to improve crime response and investigative skills, while fostering stronger relationships with communities. Efforts are also being made to enhance accountability through independent oversight and anti-corruption measures. Additionally, reforms include better pay, benefits, and mental health support for officers to improve morale and retention. While progress is being made, the success of these reforms depends on sustained political support, funding, and public involvement.

Police and Community Relations

The perception of the Jamaican police is generally negative, both within the country and internationally, due to issues of corruption, inefficiency, and strained relationships with the public. Many Jamaicans view the police with skepticism, shaped by media reports of misconduct, excessive force, and unaccountable behavior, leading to a lack of trust in the institution. This is further compounded by problems such as understaffing, limited resources, and slow response times.

Internationally, the Jamaican police are often seen as ineffective and corrupt, especially in the context of organized crime and high crime rates. Tourists may not always have direct negative experiences, but they are aware of the reputation for violence in certain areas. Despite these challenges, the JCF is working on improving its image through community policing, professional training, and anti-corruption measures, though rebuilding trust remains a slow and difficult process.

The use of police force is a significant issue in Jamaica, with concerns surrounding police brutality, excessive use of force, and extrajudicial killings frequently making headlines. Many citizens report incidents of harassment, physical abuse, and unjustified violence at the hands of law enforcement officers. This issue has contributed to a deep sense of mistrust between the Jamaican public and the police force, undermining the effectiveness of law enforcement and public cooperation.

The Independent Commission of Investigations (INDECOM), which serves as the oversight body for the police and military, has received numerous complaints related to police misconduct, including unlawful killings, beatings, and intimidation. Despite efforts to address these issues, such as calls for greater accountability, training, and oversight, the problem persists. In some cases, viral videos of police abuses, such as the controversial incident involving officers restraining an 11-year-old boy in St. Mary, have sparked public outcry and calls for reform.[13]

Although not all officers are involved in such conduct, the ongoing prevalence of these issues raises serious questions about the need for police reform in Jamaica, including better training on human rights, de-escalation tactics, and more effective mechanisms for holding officers accountable for their actions.

 ## Law of the Land True Story[14]

A recent article in The Gleaner, one of Jamaica's most prominent and long-established newspapers in the Caribbean, titled "Police's Roughhouse Tactics Not to Be Condoned, Says Senior Judge," addresses the troubling use of excessive force by law enforcement officers in Jamaica. In a recent statement, High Court Justice Bertram Morrison addressed the issue of police brutality, warning law enforcement officers not to abuse their authority by harassing or assaulting citizens. The judge's remarks came during his summation in the trial of Gregory Roberts, accused of the 2017 murder of 15-year-old schoolgirl Shineka Gray. Justice Morrison emphasized that such "roughhouse tactics" are unacceptable in civil society and undermine public trust in the police. He pointed out that these tactics not only violate human rights but also hinder the cooperation of citizens in law enforcement, as people are less likely to assist the police when they feel intimidated or abused. While acknowledging that not all police officers engage in such behavior, he stressed that the problem persists and must be addressed.

Morrison's comments followed the testimony of a civilian witness who claimed she had been beaten by the police in Dumfries. The

---

13 https://northcoasttimesja.com/
    police-and-the-11-year-old-boy/#google_vignette

14 https://jamaica-gleaner.com/article/news/20240125/
    polices-roughhouse-tactics-not-be-condoned-says-senior-judge

witness, who had initially failed to appear in court, explained that the police were more focused on physical intimidation than conducting investigations. Morrison used this example to highlight the damaging impact of police misconduct, noting that although the witness didn't report the incident to the Independent Commission of Investigations (INDECOM), it raised concerns about how such actions affect public cooperation. The issue of police brutality remains a significant national problem, with INDECOM frequently receiving complaints of abuse and extrajudicial killings by officers. This case serves as a reminder of the ongoing need for accountability and reform within the Jamaican police force.

HOW TO GET LEGAL HELP IN JAMAICA

HOW TO GET LEGAL HELP IN JAMAICA

Available Resources

If you are an American visiting Jamaica and find yourself arrested, the first and most vital contact is the U.S. Embassy in Kingston. The U.S. Embassy can provide assistance to U.S. citizens arrested in Jamaica. They can help by ensuring that your rights are respected, providing a list of local attorneys, and offering consular support. The embassy can also help in cases of wrongful detention. You can contact them at:

142 Old Hope Road, Kingston 6
Phone: (876) 702-6000
Emergency after-hours: (876) 927-5110
Website: U.S. Embassy Jamaica

The embassy can help you find a local lawyer. It is critical to have legal representation as soon as possible to ensure your rights are upheld and to navigate the Jamaican legal system.

As a foreign national arrested in Jamaica, you have several important rights. You have the right to legal representation, and if you cannot afford a lawyer, you may be eligible for legal aid. You also have the right to consular assistance, meaning you can contact your embassy for support and advice. You must be brought before a court within 48 hours of your arrest to determine if there is enough evidence to hold you in custody or release you on bail. You also have the right to remain silent during questioning, you can request to contact family or friends to inform them of your situation, and if needed, an interpreter will be provided.

Additional resource is the Jamaican Bar Association which can assist by helping you find a qualified lawyer who can represent you. They maintain a directory of licensed attorneys specializing in various areas of law, including criminal defense. While the JBA itself does not provide direct legal representation, they can refer you to a lawyer who can advise you on your rights, assist with your defense, and help navigate the legal process. Additionally, the JBA can provide guidance if you experience any issues with your lawyer or need to file complaints about legal misconduct. You can contact JBA at 876-967-1528 or via jambar.org/

Legal Aid

As a foreign detainee in Jamaica, you are generally not automatically eligible for legal aid, as it is typically reserved for Jamaican nationals or residents who cannot afford to pay for legal representation. However, if you can demonstrate that you are unable to afford legal representation, you may apply for legal aid through the Legal Aid Council in Jamaica, which reviews cases on an individual basis. The eligibility criteria include factors such as income, the nature of the offense, and the seriousness of the charge.

Even if you don't qualify for legal aid, you still have the right to consult with a lawyer. The Jamaican Bar Association can help you find a private attorney, and your embassy can assist in connecting you with legal representation. While legal aid might not be guaranteed for foreign nationals, you are entitled to a fair trial, legal representation, and consular assistance from your embassy.

Foreign Embassies in Jamaica

The mission of all embassies in Jamaica is to advance the interests of its particular country and to serve and protect its citizens either visiting or residing in the country. They offer consular assistance to individuals who are arrested or detained, ensuring their rights are upheld, providing information on legal processes, and helping connect them with local attorneys. In emergencies, such as natural disasters or civil unrest, embassies help with evacuation, safety information, and family contact. They can also issue replacement passports or travel documents for citizens. Additionally, embassies offer notarial services and work to ensure that their nationals are treated fairly under local laws, intervening if there are concerns about mistreatment.

Jamaica hosts 28 embassies and high commissions, in addition to 47 consulates. Here is a list of a few foreign embassies in Jamaica (the full list can be accessed at https://www.embassypages.com/jamaica):

The U.S. Embassy

142 Old Hope Road; Kingston 6, Jamaica, West Indies
Tel: 876-702-6000
Fax: 876-702-6348
https://jm.usembassy.gov/
Email: KingstonACS@state.gov

The Brazilian Embassy

23 Millsborough Crescent; Kingston 6, Jamaica, West Indies
Tel: 876-946-9812
Fax: 876-927-5897
http://kingston.itamaraty.gov.br/en-us/

The Canadian Embassy

3 West Kings House Road; Kingston, Jamaica
Tel: 876-926-1500
Fax: 876-733-3493
https://www.canadainternational.gc.ca/jamaica-jamaique/

Embassy of the Federal Republic of Germany

Jamaica 10 Waterloo Road; P.O. Box 444; Kingston 10 Jamaica
Mobile: 876-819-4351
Fax: 876-620-5457
https://www.german-embassy.com/de/Germany-Mission-Kingston

Italian Honorary Consulate in Kingston, Jamaica

131 Tower Street; Kingston, Jamaica
Tel: 876-948-8973 & 876-362-4771
https://www.embassypages.com/missions/embassy17422/

Russian Embassy

22 Norbrook Drive; Kingston 8, Jamaica
Tel: 876-924-1048
Fax: 876-925-8290
https://www.embassypages.com/missions/embassy17436/

High Commission of the United Kingdom

28 Trafalgar Road; Kingston 10, Jamaica (PO Box 575)
Local Tel: 876-510-0700
International: 876-510-0700
https://embassy-finder.com/united-kingdom_in_kingston_jamaica
Email: bhc.kingston@fco.gov.uk
Website: http://ukinjamaica.fco.gov.uk

MEDICAL FACILITIES & HOSPITALS

MEDICAL FACILITIES & HOSPITALS

Overview

Healthcare in Jamaica operates through a two-tier system, consisting of both public and private healthcare sectors. The public sector is government-funded, offering services that are more accessible and affordable, while the private sector provides higher-quality care at a higher cost.

The **public healthcare system** in Jamaica provides accessible and affordable care, especially in rural areas where private healthcare options may be limited. Public hospitals like Kingston Public Hospital and the University Hospital of the West Indies offer a range of services, from emergency care to specialized treatments. However, these facilities are often overcrowded and understaffed, leading to longer wait times, limited resources, and occasional delays in treatment. Although the staff in public institutions is generally qualified, the system struggles with insufficient funding, outdated equipment, and a lack of modern technologies in some cases. This can affect the overall quality of care, especially for non-emergency or elective procedures. In rural areas, access to well-trained medical professionals and adequate healthcare facilities can be more challenging.

On the other hand, the **private healthcare sector** offers higher standards of care, with modern equipment, shorter wait times, and internationally trained doctors and specialists. Private hospitals and clinics in major cities like Kingston, Montego Bay, and Ocho Rios provide high-quality treatment that is often on par with international standards. These private facilities tend to be better staffed and more equipped than public ones, but the cost can be prohibitively expensive for some visitors or locals without insurance.

In terms of staffing and training, while many healthcare workers in Jamaica are well-trained, especially in private facilities and leading public hospitals, the country does face challenges with staff shortages, particularly in rural areas. Efforts to train and retain medical professionals are ongoing, but the system still struggles with gaps in certain specialties.

Visitors' Access to Healthcare in Jamaica

If you're feeling unwell or have a medical emergency, you can seek care by visiting a clinic or hospital directly, or you can call an ambulance at **110** for urgent assistance. It's important to carry **travel insurance** to cover any medical expenses you may incur during your stay, as this will make accessing care easier and more affordable.

Foreign visitors to Jamaica have access to both public and private healthcare services, though the experience and costs can vary significantly between the two. Private healthcare is often the preferred choice for tourists, offering faster, higher-quality care with shorter waiting times and more advanced facilities, primarily located in major urban areas. However, services at these facilities come at a cost, and visitors are expected to pay upfront.

In contrast, public healthcare in Jamaica is available to foreign visitors as well, and services are generally affordable, with some treatment being free or low-cost. Public hospitals and clinics are spread across the island, but these facilities can be overcrowded, especially in urban centers, and there may be longer wait times for treatment. The quality of care in the public system can vary, and rural areas may have more limited services.

If you require emergency medical care in Jamaica, it is advisable to seek medical attention in Kingston or Montego Bay, where the healthcare infrastructure is more advanced. Emergency ambulance services are available in Kingston and can be reached at 876-978-2327, 876-978-6021, or 876-923-7415.

For additional support, the U.S. Embassy provides valuable resources, including access to information on medical evacuation providers through its Medical Assistance website. This can help ensure timely and appropriate medical evacuation if necessary.

Medical Travel Insurance

Foreign visitors to Jamaica are strongly encouraged to have **travel medical insurance** to cover any potential healthcare needs during their stay. This type of insurance generally includes coverage for emergency medical treatment, hospitalization, medical evacuation, and in some cases, repatriation of remains. Many travel insurance plans also offer coverage for unexpected medical costs, such as doctor's visits, medications, and even lost luggage or trip interruptions, which could impact a visitor's ability to access healthcare.

When it comes to out-of-pocket costs, private healthcare in Jamaica can be relatively expensive, especially for emergency care or specialized treatment. Costs can vary widely based on the type of service received, but typical expenses might include consultation fees, emergency room visits, diagnostic tests, and treatment. For example, a general consultation at a private clinic might cost between US$40 to US$100, while more extensive services such as surgery or hospitalization can run into the hundreds or thousands of dollars, depending on the complexity.

The cost of travel medical insurance to Jamaica varies depending on several factors, including the duration of your stay, your age, your health condition, the level of coverage you require, and the provider you choose. On average, travel medical insurance for a short stay (e.g., 7 to 14 days) typically costs between US$30 to $100 per person. For longer stays, or if you need more comprehensive coverage that includes medical evacuation, trip cancellation, or coverage for pre-existing conditions, the cost can range from US$150 to $400 or more.

The cost also increases with age or if you have any pre-existing health conditions, as insurers may charge more for higher-risk travelers.

To get the best deal and ensure adequate coverage, it's advisable to compare quotes from different insurance providers before purchasing a plan. Additionally, check that the plan covers medical emergencies, hospital stays, evacuation, and repatriation to your home country in case of a severe illness or injury.

 For more information on travel medical insurance, tips and quote comparisons, visit **https://www.squaremouth.com/destinations/jamaica**.

 As you travel to Jamaica, keep these emergency numbers at hand:

- **Police:** 119
- **Ambulance/Medical Emergency:** 110
- **Fire Department:** 110
- **National Disaster Emergency:** 1-888-776-7634

Medical Facilities

There are approximately 30 to 40 hospitals and clinics operating across the island. Most of these institutions fall under the public sector. However, the quality of service can vary significantly among these hospitals. In many areas, particularly outside the capital, Kingston, individuals may have to travel long distances for adequate care as advanced emergency services are typically available in more urbanized regions. Only Kingston offers comprehensive medical care, which highlights the geographical disparities in healthcare access across the island.[15]

---

15 https://expatfinancial.com/healthcare-information-by-region/
   caribbean-healthcare-system/jamaica-healthcare-system

As of recent data, the healthcare workforce in Jamaica has seen some improvements. The cadre of doctors in the country has increased from 1,507 to 2,089, while the number of nurses has slightly risen from 4,669 to 4,741.[16] Additionally, other healthcare professionals, such as community health aides and nursing professionals, play significant roles in delivering healthcare services. In 2016, there were about 3,201 nursing professionals.[17] These figures demonstrate an ongoing effort to strengthen the healthcare workforce, although challenges remain regarding the adequacy of staffing to meet the population's needs.

Overall, medical facilities in Jamaica have improved significantly over the years, making the country a favorable destination for medical tourism. Notably, several hospitals and clinics stand out for their quality of care, range of services, and reputation among travelers:

- **University Hospital of the West Indies:** One of the leading medical institutions in Jamaica, the hospital has held its ground as a reliable facility for both locals and tourists. Located in Kingston, the hospital is affiliated with the University College of the West Indies and serves as a teaching hospital. Established in 1948, UHWI provides a wide variety of specialized medical services, including trauma care, general surgery, and emergency medicine. With experienced medical professionals and advanced medical technology, UHWI is a trusted choice for foreign travelers seeking comprehensive healthcare services.

- **Kingston Public Hospital:** As the largest public hospital on the island, Kingston Public Hospital (KPH) offers extensive healthcare services to both local and foreign patients. KPH is known for its commitment to cater to emergencies, surgery, maternity care, and general medicine. Although it primarily serves Jamaican citizens, travelers have access to its emergency and hospital services. The facility's strategic location in the capital means it can handle a high volume of patients and various medical conditions

---

16 https://jamaica-gleaner.com/article/lead-stories/20250120/
    plans-under-way-make-placement-long-scorned-regions-more-palatable

17 https://jamaica.tracking-progress.org/
    indicator/3-c-1b-number-of-health-workers-persons/

- **Andrews Memorial Hospital:** This private facility located in Kingston is particularly notable for conducting medical examinations required for U.S. immigrant visas. The hospital has earned a reputation for high-quality patient care, offering services like outpatient care, dental procedures, and COVID-19 testing. Its accreditation and commitment to maintaining high standards make it a suitable option for foreign visitors seeking medical services while in Jamaica.

- **Baywest Wellness Hospital:** Located in Montego Bay, the hospital aims to be a leading healthcare provider within the Jamaican private sector and is known for offering a broad spectrum of medical services. The facility is noted for providing telemedicine services. With a focus on medical tourism, Baywest has tailored its offerings to accommodate tourists by providing accessible and high-quality health services that meet international health standards.

- **Omega Medical Hospital:** Recognized for providing comprehensive healthcare services beyond standard offerings, this facility specializes in areas such as cosmetic surgery and aesthetic treatments. With 24-hour service for medical issues, Omega Medical Hospital is well-positioned to serve foreign visitors, particularly those interested in specialized treatments while enjoying their visit to Jamaica. Its commitment to patient care and a wide array of specialists appeal to many medical tourists looking for quality services.

DRIVING IN JAMAICA

IN THIS CHAPTER

- Overview
- Requirements for Foreign Drivers
- Main Traffic Rules
- Road Safety Tips
- General Questions
- Law of the Land Hypothetical

CHAPTER 18

DRIVING IN JAMAICA

Overview

Driving in Jamaica can be a unique and sometimes challenging experience, particularly for visitors unfamiliar with the island's road conditions and driving culture. The country uses **left-hand drive** (steering wheel on the right side of the vehicle), which may be disorienting for visitors from countries that drive on the right. The road network in urban areas, like Kingston and Montego Bay, is relatively well-developed, with paved roads and highways connecting key destinations. However, outside of major cities, road conditions can be less predictable, with some rural roads being narrow, poorly lit, or in disrepair.

In terms of traffic, urban areas like Kingston can experience significant congestion, especially during peak hours. While there are some modern highways, many roads are congested and filled with a mix of private cars, taxis, buses, and motorcycles. Jamaica's roadways can also be populated by pedestrians, animals, and unpredictable driving behavior, which may include aggressive overtaking, erratic lane changes, and lack of adherence to road rules in some cases. Road signs and signals are often not as visible or consistent as in other countries and driving at night can be risky due to poorly lit roads, especially in more rural areas.

On the positive side, Jamaica has a network of rental car companies that make driving accessible to tourists, and the opportunity to explore the island at your own pace can be rewarding. Visitors should drive cautiously and defensively, be prepared for rough patches of road, and take care in unfamiliar areas. It's also worth noting that local drivers, while sometimes unpredictable, are accustomed to the road conditions and can often navigate them more confidently than tourists. For those not comfortable driving, taxis and private drivers are widely available as alternatives.

Requirements for Foreign Drivers

If you plan to drive when visiting Jamaica, you should ensure you have your **national driver's license**, which is typically valid for use in Jamaica for up to 12 months. It's also a good idea to carry an **International Driving Permit (IDP)**, particularly if you're from a non-English speaking country, as it helps with any language barriers. Additionally, if you're renting a car, make sure to have your **rental agreement** and proof of insurance on hand, as these may be required in case of an accident or other incidents.

In terms of **insurance**, Jamaica has specific requirements for drivers. By law, all vehicles, including rental cars, must carry third-party liability insurance. This insurance covers any damage or injury caused to others in the event of an accident. Most car rental companies include this insurance in the rental price, but it's always wise to double-check. While third-party insurance is mandatory, you may also want to consider comprehensive insurance, which covers damage to the rental vehicle itself in case of an accident, theft, or vandalism. This is optional but highly recommended for added peace of mind, especially for visitors unfamiliar with local driving conditions. Additionally, a Collision Damage Waiver (CDW) is often offered, which waives your liability for damage to the rental car, and Personal Accident Insurance (PAI) can cover medical expenses for injuries sustained in an accident. Before driving, it's important to ensure that you have adequate coverage for both the vehicle and any potential medical emergencies.

Main Traffic Rules

Driving in Jamaica comes with its own set of traffic rules and regulations that visitors should be aware of to ensure safety and avoid legal issues. Here are some of the main traffic rules:

- **Drive on the Left**: Jamaica follows left-hand driving, meaning that the steering wheel is on the right side of the vehicle. Drivers must keep to the left side of the road at all times.

- **Seat Belts**: Seat belts are mandatory for all passengers in the vehicle, not just the driver. Failure to wear a seatbelt can result in fines or penalties.

- **Speed Limits:** Speed limits vary depending on the type of road. In urban areas, the speed limit is typically 50 km/h (31 mph), while on highways or main roads, it can go up to 80-100 km/h (50-62 mph). However, speed limits are clearly posted, and it's important to adhere to them to avoid fines and ensure safety.

- **Drinking and Driving:** The legal blood alcohol concentration (BAC) limit in Jamaica is 0.08%. Driving under the influence of alcohol or drugs is illegal and can lead to heavy fines, imprisonment, or worse, an accident.

- **Road Signs:** Jamaica uses standard international road signs, but some may not always be visible or maintained in rural areas. Be sure to pay attention to road markings, stop signs, and speed limit signs when driving.

- **Use of Mobile Phones:** It is illegal to use a mobile phone while driving unless you are using a hands-free device.

- **Overtaking:** Overtaking on the left side is prohibited unless the road is specifically designed for it. Overtake only on the right and always check for oncoming traffic before doing so.

- **Pedestrian Crossings:** Pedestrians have the right of way at designated pedestrian crossings. Drivers should always stop to allow pedestrians to cross safely.

■ **Motorcycles and Helmets:** Motorcyclists and their passengers must wear helmets at all times, and it is illegal for a motorcyclist to carry more than one passenger.

Toll roads are an important part of the island's infrastructure, designed to help maintain and improve major highways connecting key cities and tourist destinations. One of the most well-known toll roads is the North-South Highway, also known as Highway 2000, which runs from Kingston to Ocho Rios. There are also other toll routes, such as the Southern Coastal Highway, linking Kingston with the southern parts of the island.

The toll system is straightforward but requires drivers to stop at toll booths to pay fees, which vary depending on the distance traveled and the type of vehicle. For those who prefer a faster and more convenient option, the Jamaica Toll Pass is available. This electronic system uses RFID technology, allowing drivers to pay tolls without stopping, by simply passing through the toll booth, where the fee is automatically deducted from an account linked to the pass. While cash is accepted at most booths, some locations also accept credit and debit cards. The toll rates differ based on the vehicle, with smaller cars paying less than larger vehicles like trucks or buses.

For tourists and frequent travelers, the Jamaica Toll Pass is a convenient option, as it can be purchased at toll plazas or online. While toll roads can add to travel costs, they provide faster routes to popular destinations, making them a preferred choice for many visitors exploring the island.

Road Safety Tips

Road safety in Jamaica presents challenges due to a mix of driver behavior, road conditions, and public transportation issues. Reckless driving, speeding, and unsafe overtaking are common, especially in urban areas, while pedestrians often face risks due to inadequate crossings. Road quality varies; major highways are generally well-maintained, but some rural roads can be poorly lit or have potholes, especially during rainy weather. Public transportation, such as buses and taxis, sometimes involves unsafe practices like overloading and lack of seat belts. To address these issues, the National Road Safety Council works to enforce laws and raise awareness. Visitors should drive defensively, stay alert, and follow local traffic laws to ensure safety on the roads.

If you're stopped by the Jamaica Constabulary Force (JCF) while driving, stay calm and cooperative. Pull over safely to the side of the road, ideally to a well-lit area if it's dark. Remain inside your vehicle with your hands visible on the steering wheel. The officer will likely ask for your driver's license, vehicle registration, insurance documents, and possibly your passport for identification, especially if you're a foreign visitor.

Be respectful and polite, and if the officer doesn't explain the reason for the stop, politely ask. If given a fine, keep the receipt, as you can dispute it later through legal channels. Never offer a bribe, as it is illegal. If you're asked for one, report the incident to the police or your embassy. Staying calm and compliant will help ensure the situation is handled smoothly.

Here are a few road safety tips for driving in Jamaica:

- Drive on the left side of the road, as this is the standard in Jamaica.
- Be cautious on narrow, winding roads, especially in rural areas.
- Watch out for pedestrians and animals that may cross the road unexpectedly.
- Adhere to speed limits where posted but always adjust your speed according to road conditions.
- Ensure all passengers wear seat belts, as it is mandatory.
- Drive carefully at night, as roads may not be well-lit and hazards like potholes can be difficult to see.
- Pay attention to traffic signs and signals and be prepared for aggressive driving behaviors.
- If unfamiliar with the area, use a GPS or local guide for navigation.
- Always keep emergency contact numbers (police, car rental company) handy.

 **General Questions**

1. *Can I use my driver's license from my home country to drive in Jamaica?* Yes, you can use your driver's license from your home country to drive in Jamaica, as long as it is valid and written in English. Visitors can drive using their foreign driver's license for up to three months from their arrival date. If your license is not in English, it's recommended to carry an International Driving Permit (IDP) along with your original license. However, if you plan to stay longer than three months or if you're unsure, you may need to apply for a Jamaican driver's license. If renting a car, some rental agencies may also require you to present an IDP in addition to your home country license, so it's best to confirm with the rental company beforehand

2. *What is the age requirement for renting a car in Jamaica?* The minimum age to rent a car in Jamaica is typically 21 years old. However, rental agencies may impose additional requirements, such as a valid driver's license held for at least one year. Some agencies may have a higher minimum age requirement, such as 25, or charge an additional young driver fee for renters under 25. It's important to check with the specific car rental company for their policies, as requirements can vary, especially for those with less driving experience.

 **Law of the Land Hypothetical**

HYPOTHETICAL: *Amy is a U.S. citizen. She turned 18 years old last week. To celebrate, she plans to travel to Jamaica and drive around the country to sightsee and visit several cities. She is planning to rent a vehicle; will she encounter any problems?*

ANSWER: *Amy may encounter some challenges when trying to rent a car in Jamaica. Most rental agencies require drivers to be at least 21 years old, and some even have a minimum age of 25. Since she is 18, she may not meet the minimum age requirement for most companies. Additionally, if she does find a rental agency that allows drivers under 21, she may be subject to a young driver fee. It's important for Amy to check with specific car rental agencies ahead of time to understand their age policies and any additional charges that may apply.*

NUDE BEACHES & CLOTHING-OPTIONAL RESORTS

CHAPTER 19
NUDE BEACHES & CLOTHING-OPTIONAL RESORTS

Overview[18]

Jamaica stands out as a premier destination in the Caribbean, especially renowned among enthusiasts of beaches. The allure of the island is multifaceted, with its expansive beaches, tropical climate, and the relaxed ambiance heightened by the availability of ganja, creating an environment that inspires honeymooning couples and adults seeking romantic getaways.

Jamaica does not have a widespread nudist culture, and public nudity is generally not culturally acceptable, with most Jamaicans adhering to conservative social norms regarding modesty. However, the island offers some exceptions for those interested in naturism, primarily in private, clothing-optional resorts or designated beach areas that cater to tourists. These resorts, such as Hedonism II and Grand Lido in Negril, and Couples Tower Isle in Ocho Rios, provide designated spaces where nudity is allowed and legally practiced. While nudism is not widely accepted outside of these private settings, Jamaica's tourism industry supports a more inclusive environment in these specific locations. Visitors should be mindful of local laws and customs, ensuring they enjoy nudist activities in appropriate, legal spaces.

---

18 https://sandee.com/blog/nudism-laws-in-jamaica

Legality

Nudism in Jamaica is regulated, primarily through its laws governing public behavior and decency. Public nudity, including nudism on beaches, is generally illegal in Jamaica, and anyone caught engaging in public nudity can face legal consequences, including fines or other penalties. The country maintains a conservative stance on public decency, with most Jamaicans adhering to traditional values of modesty.

However, there are exceptions for nudist activities in private spaces, particularly in designated clothing-optional resorts and private beaches. These resorts, which cater to tourists, are allowed to provide areas where nudity is accepted and legally permitted. Nudism is only regulated and allowed in these controlled, private environments, where guests are free to enjoy clothing-free experiences within the boundaries of the resort or beach. Visitors must ensure they are in these designated areas to comply with local laws while enjoying their nudist activities.

Jamaica offers several well-known resorts and beaches that cater to naturists and those seeking a clothing-optional experience. Here are some of the most popular and renowned ones:

1. **Hedonism II (Negril).** Located in Negril, Hedonism II is one of the most famous adult-only resorts with a dedicated nudist beach. It's an all-inclusive resort offering a range of activities for those looking for a clothing-optional environment. The resort features both nude and non-nude areas, ensuring guests can enjoy the freedom of naturism in a safe and private setting.

2. **Grand Lido (Negril).** Grand Lido is another well-regarded resort in Negril with a private nude beach area. It provides a luxurious, clothing-optional experience, where guests can enjoy the natural beauty of the island in a relaxed and secure environment. The resort is known for its upscale accommodations, excellent service, and nude-friendly amenities.

3. **Couples Tower Isle (Ocho Rios).** Situated in Ocho Rios, Couples Tower Isle offers a private island for its guests, where clothing-optional sunbathing and swimming are allowed. This resort is known

for its intimate atmosphere and provides a high-end experience for those looking to embrace the naturist lifestyle while enjoying all-inclusive amenities.

4. **Seven Mile Beach (Negril).** While not an official nude beach, Seven Mile Beach in Negril is known for being a more relaxed and tolerant area for naturists, with some resorts offering private sections for clothing-optional activities. Many visitors to this iconic stretch of beach choose to go without clothing in certain areas, though it's important to respect the designated spaces and local rules.

5. **Desire Resort (Negril).** Located in Negril, Desire Resort offers a clothing-optional atmosphere. It's a luxury resort designed for adults and is known for its vibrant and open-minded vibe. The resort's secluded atmosphere makes it an ideal spot for naturists to unwind and enjoy a private beach experience.

Nudist Etiquette and Safety

When visiting Jamaica and participating in nudist activities, it's important to observe certain etiquette to ensure a respectful and enjoyable experience for everyone. First and foremost, always stay within designated clothing-optional areas. In these naturist environments, respecting privacy is key—never take photos of others without their consent and avoid making others uncomfortable with inappropriate behavior or comments.

Another important aspect of nudist etiquette is maintaining respect for the communal space. When walking around shared areas like restaurants, pools, or shops, it's courteous to bring a towel or cover-up to maintain a sense of modesty. Additionally, practicing good hygiene is essential, particularly in places like pools or hot tubs. Finally, always engage with others in a respectful manner—if someone prefers to be left alone, it's important to respect their space and avoid unwanted interactions. By following these guidelines, visitors can enjoy Jamaica's naturist offerings while being mindful of the local culture and ensuring a positive environment for everyone.

Safety is an important consideration when visiting nudist beaches in Jamaica, as with any type of vacation or leisure activity. While Jamaica offers some fantastic, designated clothing-optional resorts and beaches, it's essential to follow a few safety guidelines to ensure a safe and enjoyable experience.

First, always stick to the designated naturist areas to avoid legal issues. Public nudity outside these areas is illegal, and staying within the approved spaces helps prevent any legal consequences. Secondly, it's important to be mindful of your personal belongings. On beaches, it's advisable not to leave valuables unattended, as theft can sometimes be an issue, especially in more secluded or less crowded areas. Many resorts provide safe storage options for guests' valuables, so take advantage of those.

When it comes to personal safety, protect yourself from the sun. The Jamaican sun can be intense, so ensure you're using a high SPF sunscreen and take regular breaks in the shade to avoid sunburn. Hydration is also key, especially if you're spending a long time outdoors. For your health and hygiene, always bring a towel to sit on, particularly when using shared spaces like lounges or pools, and follow the resort's hygiene guidelines for communal areas.

Finally, always keep an eye on the water conditions when at the beach. Like any beach destination, some areas may have stronger currents or waves, so follow any posted safety warnings and listen to lifeguards or resort staff if they offer guidance.

? General Questions

1. *What is the most renowned nude beach in Jamaica, and what should I know before visiting?* Hedonism II in Negril is Jamaica's most renowned nude beach and clothing-optional resort, offering a private, adult-only environment where guests can enjoy a naturist experience on designated nude beaches. The resort provides all-inclusive amenities, themed parties, and a vibrant social atmosphere, making it popular among couples, singles, and groups seeking a relaxed, body-positive space. While nudity is welcomed in these private areas, it's important to respect local laws and avoid public nudity outside the resort. Visitors should be aware of the resort's respectful code of conduct and secure their personal belongings while enjoying the freedom the resort offers.

2. *What should I wear when visiting a nude beach in Jamaica, and is it necessary to bring anything specific?* When visiting a nude beach in Jamaica, you can enjoy the freedom of nudity in designated areas. Outside of these zones, however, you'll need to cover up with appropriate clothing like a cover-up or swimsuit. Bring a towel or beach mat to sit on, sunscreen, sunglasses, and a hat for sun protection. It's also important to secure your valuables, as these beaches may not have typical amenities for personal security.

 **Law of the Land Hypothetical**

HYPOTHETICAL: *Jane is happy to be traveling to Jamaica because she can finally work on her tan for an entire week. Shortly after settling in, Jane travels to a public beach, takes off her clothes, and lies down face up on her beach towel. Is Jane violating Jamaican law?*

ANSWER: *Yes, Jane is violating Jamaican law. Public nudity is illegal in Jamaica, and while there are designated clothing-optional areas at specific resorts and private beaches, public beaches are not among them. By removing her clothes on a public beach, Jane is engaging in behavior that is not culturally or legally acceptable outside of designated zones. She should ensure she is in a private, clothing-optional resort or beach area, such as those in Negril, where nudity is permitted, to avoid any legal issues.*

CHAPTER 20
UNUSUAL LAWS

UNUSUAL LAWS

Overview

Unusual laws can be fascinating glimpses into a culture's values and history. While most people are aware of common legal restrictions, it's often the strange and quirky laws that capture our attention. These regulations can range from the amusing to the absurd, reflecting the unique circumstances and traditions of a place. Whether they arise from historical events, societal norms, or simply peculiar local customs, unusual laws can provide insight into the quirks of human behavior and governance.

Jamaica's collection of quirky and unusual laws serves as a testament to its rich heritage, reflecting historical norms, cultural practices, and societal values that have shaped the nation. While many of these laws may seem outdated or bizarre by contemporary standards, they offer a fascinating glimpse into the complexities of Jamaican society. Here are a few of such laws:

- It is illegal to empty a privy (outdoor toilet) between the hours of 4 am and 10 pm, a law originating from older sanitation practices aimed at maintaining public hygiene and decency.

- Shaking or beating a mat is prohibited after 8 am, except for doormats, to control noise and maintain peace in the community.

- Getting married after 6 pm is illegal, reflecting a historical preference for conducting weddings during daylight hours.

- It is also illegal to sell rope after 6 pm, although the rationale behind this law is unclear.

- It is illegal to ring someone's doorbell without a lawful reason, emphasizing respect for personal space and privacy.

- It's illegal to engage in public displays of affection, such as kissing or hugging, on Sundays which is said to be tied to the island's historical colonial-era regulations around public decency. However, it's more of a cultural norm than a strictly enforced law.

- It's illegal to wear ragged or torn clothing in public. This law was designed to maintain a sense of public decency, though it's not strictly enforced today.

- Under the Jamaican Bicycle Act, it is illegal to sell, purchase, or even repair a second-hand bicycle without a license and payment of the appropriate license fee.

Penalties and Fines

It should be mentioned that many of these laws are relics of older times, and while they still technically exist, they are not actively enforced today unless they are part of a broader public health or nuisance control issue. In general, these laws serve as historical curiosities more than practical regulations in modern Jamaican society. However, breaches related to public decency, noise, or disturbance might attract fines under other general public order laws.

It's highly unlikely that you would be fined or penalized for breaking any of these archaic laws in Jamaica today. The only law that might attract some attention is the one involving the sale or repair of second-hand bicycles, as it relates to business regulations and licensing. In that case, there could be fines, especially if you're operating without the required license, but this is specific to the trade of bicycles rather than a personal, everyday action.

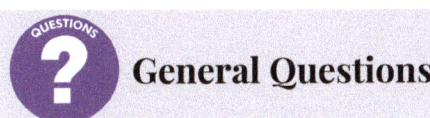

General Questions

1. *Is it illegal to wear camouflage clothing in Jamaica?* Yes. Camouflage is the official uniform of the Jamaica Defense Force and so, to avoid confusing a civilian for a member of law enforcement, the wearing of camouflage is prohibited. Break the law and you could face up to $2,000 or more in fines or possibly serve some jail time.

2. *Is there a law in Jamaica that restricts the sale of alcohol at certain times?* Yes, Jamaica has laws that restrict the sale of alcohol after certain hours, particularly in specific areas. In some regions, it is illegal to sell alcohol after 11 PM, with exceptions made for certain establishments like hotels or licensed bars. The rationale behind this law is to promote public order and reduce the potential for disturbances late at night. While this law is still technically in place, its enforcement can vary depending on the location and type of establishment. In tourist areas, for example, you may find that some businesses operate under special licenses allowing them to serve alcohol later into the night. Nonetheless, this restriction serves as a reminder of the country's historical approach to controlling nightlife and promoting public safety.

3. *Is it illegal to operate businesses on Sundays, Christmas Day, and Boxing Day?* Yes, under Section 16 of the Towns and Communities Act, all businesses are required to close on Sundays, or their owners may face legal consequences. However, there are exceptions: pharmacies are allowed to operate between 8 AM and 12 midnight on Sundays, as well as on Christmas Day and Good Friday, for the sale of drugs. Shops within the two major airports, businesses that cater to travelers, and establishments selling motor fuel (gas) are also exempt from this restriction. Additionally, businesses selling bread or ice, public markets, and newspaper printing establishments are allowed to remain open. However, newspaper printers can only operate between 10 AM and 5 PM on these days. Violating this law can result in a fine of $20 or imprisonment for up to 30 days.

 **Law of the Land Hypothetical**

HYPOTHETICAL: *What might happen if someone decides to get married after 6 PM in Jamaica, even though it's technically illegal?*

ANSWER: *While this law still technically exists, it is largely outdated and not enforced in modern Jamaica. In practice, the couple would not face any legal repercussions for having their wedding after 6 PM. The officer might offer a gentle reminder of the law's historical significance, but it's highly unlikely that any fines or penalties would be imposed. Given that the law is no longer relevant and not enforced, the wedding would proceed without further issues. The couple would probably laugh it off as an old and quirky regulation that no longer applies to their day-to-day life.*

TRAVELING SAFELY

IN THIS CHAPTER

- Ladies Traveling Solo
- Traveling as a Family
- Do's and Don'ts While in Jamaica

TRAVELING SAFELY

Ladies Traveling Solo

Jamaica is generally considered safe for tourists, particularly in popular tourist areas such as Montego Bay, Negril, Ocho Rios, and the North Coast. These areas are well-established for tourism, with numerous resorts, attractions, and significant investments in security to ensure the safety of visitors. Many tourists enjoy the island's natural beauty, rich culture, and vibrant entertainment with no to minimal issues. Nevertheless, some governments, including the United States, issue occasional travel advisories for specific regions of Jamaica, typically recommending that travelers avoid certain neighborhoods due to safety concerns. This often applies more to Kingston or areas with gang activity rather than popular tourist spots.

Jamaica can be safe for a woman traveling by herself, but like any destination, it requires awareness and precautions. While many solo female travelers visit and enjoy the island, it's important to take steps to ensure your safety, particularly when navigating areas outside the main tourist zones.

Safety Tips for Solo Female Travelers in Jamaica

Popular tourist destinations like Montego Bay, Negril, Ocho Rios, and Port Antonio are generally safe for solo female travelers. These areas are well-patrolled, with a strong police presence, private security at resorts, and lots of other tourists, which helps create a safer environment. Avoid venturing into unfamiliar or high-crime areas, especially after dark.

Avoid hailing taxis off the street. Instead, use reputable taxi services, or arrange transportation through your hotel or resort. Private shuttles or tourist buses are safer options for traveling around the island.

It's generally safer to avoid walking alone at night, particularly in less populated or poorly lit areas. Stick to your hotel or well-populated spots after dark and take advantage of hotel transportation or taxis.

Petty crime like pickpocketing and bag-snatching can happen in busy tourist areas, so it's important to keep your valuables secure. Use a money belt or a hotel safe for important items like passports, cash, and credit cards.

As with traveling anywhere, trust your instincts. If a situation feels uncomfortable or if you feel unsafe, remove yourself from the area. Jamaican people are generally warm and welcoming, but it's still important to exercise caution when interacting with strangers.

Jamaicans are generally friendly, but you may encounter some unwanted attention from local men, especially in tourist areas. A polite but firm response, or simply walking away, is often the best way to handle it. If you ever feel uncomfortable, don't hesitate to seek help from hotel staff or trusted locals.

Choose well-reviewed and reputable accommodations, ideally with strong security measures in place (e.g., 24-hour reception, security cameras, and guards). Many upscale resorts offer a great deal of safety for solo travelers.

Traveling as a Family

Traveling to Jamaica with children can be an exciting and memorable experience, but it's important to take certain safety and health precautions to ensure a smooth and enjoyable trip.

Choosing a family-friendly resort is a great first step. Resorts in places like Montego Bay, Negril, and Ocho Rios often cater to families, providing amenities such as childcare, kids' clubs, and supervised activities. These resorts typically have higher levels of security and are well-equipped to handle families. Once you're settled, it's crucial to ensure safe transportation. Using reliable options like hotel shuttles or reputable taxi services and making sure your child is safely secured in a child safety seat, is key. Public transportation may not always be the safest or most comfortable option for families, so it's best to avoid it.

While enjoying the beautiful Jamaican beaches and resorts, it's important to keep a close eye on your children, particularly around water, as some areas can have strong currents. Many beaches have lifeguards, but it's always safer to stay vigilant and use swim vests for younger or less confident swimmers. Always have essentials on hand, such as snacks, water, medications, and sun protection. A first-aid kit with band-aids, antiseptic wipes, and necessary medications is a must. It's also wise to be aware of local safety concerns. Stick to well-populated tourist-friendly areas and avoid wandering into unfamiliar neighborhoods, especially after dark. Teaching your children about personal boundaries and being cautious with strangers is also important to ensure their safety.

Health precautions are another key aspect of traveling with children. Make sure everyone in the family is up to date on routine vaccinations like MMR, DTaP, and polio. Some additional vaccinations, such as Hepatitis A, Hepatitis B, Typhoid, and Malaria, may be recommended depending on where you plan to go and the type of activities you'll be doing. Consult your doctor well in advance to ensure you're fully prepared. Jamaica's tropical climate means strong sun exposure, so always apply broad-spectrum sunscreen generously on your children's skin and reapply regularly. Protecting them with hats, sunglasses, and light clothing will help shield them from the sun's intensity, and make sure they stay hydrated by drinking plenty of water.

To avoid stomach issues, stick to bottled water instead of tap water and avoid ice unless it's made from purified water. Stick to well-cooked food and be cautious about eating street food. Wash hands frequently and use hand sanitizers before meals. Mosquitoes in Jamaica can carry diseases like Dengue fever and Zika virus, so apply mosquito repellent containing

DEET to your children, especially during early mornings and evenings. If possible, dress them in long sleeves and pants to further reduce exposure. Ensure your accommodation has screened windows and air conditioning to keep insects out.

Finally, it's essential to check that your travel insurance covers medical care for your children while abroad. Familiarize yourself with local emergency numbers and know the location of the nearest hospital or medical center. If your child takes prescription medication, make sure to bring enough for the duration of the trip, keeping it in its original packaging. It's a good idea to carry a doctor's note explaining the medication in case you need to show it at customs or airport security.

 **Safety Tips**

Here are a few key safety tips for traveling with family:

- Keep family members close, especially in crowded or unfamiliar areas, with a designated "buddy" to minimize the risk of anyone getting lost.

- Delegate tasks like carrying important documents or valuables to different family members.

- Set up clear meeting spots in case anyone temporarily splits up, ensuring quick reunification.

- Stay connected using mobile phones and location-sharing apps to track each other's whereabouts.

- Stay alert in crowded areas, hold onto belongings, and watch out for pickpockets.

- Learn about Jamaican cultural norms to avoid misunderstandings and show respect.

- Reach out to local officials or hotel staff if you need assistance or have concerns.

- Educate kids on basic safety rules, such as the buddy system and not talking to strangers.

- Get advice on safe local attractions and activities tailored to families.

- Know emergency contacts and carry a first-aid kit and necessary medications.

- If something feels off, prioritize your family's safety and take appropriate action.

Do's and Don'ts While in Jamaica

When visiting Jamaica, it's important to embrace local customs while at the same time be mindful of your surroundings to ensure a respectful and enjoyable trip. Here's a dos and don'ts to guide your visit:

- **Do greet people warmly** with a smile or a friendly "hello," as Jamaicans are known for their hospitality. However, **don't take photos without asking permission**, especially of locals or in rural areas, as it can be seen as intrusive.

- **Do try the local cuisine**, like jerk chicken or ackee and saltfish, but **don't engage in drug-related activities**, as Jamaica has strict laws about illegal drugs, despite the decriminalization of small amounts of marijuana for personal use.

- **Do stay hydrated and wear sunscreen** to protect against the intense tropical sun, but **don't wear swimwear outside of the beach** or pool areas, as it's considered disrespectful in public places like shops and restaurants.

- **Do use reliable transportation options**, such as hotel shuttles or licensed taxis, for added safety. **Don't rely on public transport**

in unfamiliar areas, as it may be overcrowded or less secure for tourists.

- **Do keep your belongings secure** and be cautious in busy areas, but **don't wear expensive jewelry** in public, as it could attract unwanted attention.

- **Do participate in local activities** like cultural festivals or guided tours, but **don't engage in loud public disputes**, as public arguments can be viewed as aggressive or rude.

- **Do tip for good service** in hotels, restaurants, and with local guides, as tipping is customary, but **don't flash large amounts of cash** or valuables, especially in crowded or unfamiliar areas.

- **Do ask questions if you need help**, whether from locals or hotel staff, as Jamaicans are generally friendly and willing to assist, but **don't take unnecessary risks in unfamiliar places**—stick to well-populated tourist areas, especially at night.

TOURIST TAXATION

- Tourist Taxes in Jamaica
- Law of the Land Hypothetical

TOURIST TAXATION

Tourist Taxes in Jamaica

Jamaica has a few tourist-related taxes that visitors should be aware of when planning their trip. Jamaica charges tourist taxes as a way to sustain and enhance the country's tourism infrastructure, which is vital to its economy. Tourism is one of the largest contributors to Jamaica's national income, so the government uses these taxes to improve the services and facilities that tourists rely on. For example, the funds collected help maintain and upgrade airports, roads, and transportation systems that ensure smooth travel experiences. The money also goes towards preserving Jamaica's natural beauty—beaches, coral reefs, and national parks—so the country remains an attractive destination for visitors.

Additionally, these taxes help fund public services that both locals and tourists depend on, such as healthcare and security, particularly in high-traffic tourist areas. The funds also support sustainable tourism initiatives, ensuring that growth in the sector doesn't come at the expense of the environment. By using tourist taxes to reinvest in the country, Jamaica can improve the overall quality of its tourism products, whether that's upgrading accommodations, enhancing local attractions, or investing in new tourism ventures.

Here are the main tourist taxes in Jamaica:

1. Accommodation Tax

This tax is levied on accommodation stays in hotels, guesthouses, villas, and other types of lodgings. The rate varies depending on the classification of the property:

- For properties charging **up to J$2,000 per night**, the tax is **US$0.50** (approximately).

- For properties charging **over J$2,000 per night**, the tax is **US$1** per room per night.

- For higher-end properties (like resorts or luxury hotels), this may be more, depending on the pricing of the room.

2. Tourism Development Tax (TDL)

This is a fixed tax applied to accommodation bookings, which is **US$1 per night** for all foreign visitors staying at accommodations in Jamaica. The tax is automatically included in the booking cost, and you will typically see it listed separately on your bill.

3. Departure Tax

When leaving Jamaica, there is a departure tax (also called the Passenger Service Charge), which covers airport services and maintenance. It is typically included in the price of your airline ticket for international flights. However, if not included in your ticket, you may need to pay this tax at the airport: **US$35** for international departures.

4. Environmental Tax

Some tourist attractions, like national parks or excursions, may have an environmental or entry fee. These fees go toward preserving Jamaica's natural resources and protecting the local environment. The amounts can vary widely, depending on the attraction.

5. Value-Added Tax (VAT)

Jamaica has a **15% VAT**, which is added to goods and services, including tourism-related purchases such as meals at restaurants, car rentals, or souvenirs. The VAT is typically included in the price you pay, so you won't need to calculate this separately.

6. Airport Security Tax

When flying out of Jamaica, there may be a small security tax of **around US$2**, which can be included in the cost of your flight or payable separately at the airport, depending on the airline.

 **Law of the Land Hypothetical**

HYPOTHETICAL: *David and his family have decided to spend their holiday at a luxurious five-star resort in Ocho Rios, Jamaica. After checking in and getting settled into their oceanfront villa, he notices some additional charges on their bill for Tourism Development Levy and Accommodation Tax. Curious about these extra fees, David calls the front desk to get more information.*

ANSWER: *The staff explains that the Tourism Development Levy is a US$2 per night charge, used to improve tourism infrastructure like airports and attractions. The Accommodation Tax is based on the room price, with David's premium villa incurring a US$3 per night fee. These taxes are applied to all tourists, regardless of the resort's price, and help maintain Jamaica's tourism services and facilities. David learns that the funds from these taxes ensure the island remains a top destination for visitors.*

LONG-TERM STAYS

IN THIS CHAPTER

- Overview
- Long-Term Visas
- Residency Requirements for Foreigners
- General Questions
- Law of the Land Hypothetical
- Law of the Land True Story

CHAPTER 23
LONG-TERM STAYS

Overview

Many people choose to stay long-term in Jamaica for its natural beauty, affordable cost of living, and vibrant culture. The island's stunning beaches, mountains, and tropical climate attract those seeking a slower pace of life, while its lower cost of living—especially outside tourist areas—makes it an appealing option for retirees and expats. Jamaica's rich cultural heritage, friendly locals, and tax incentives for retirees further enhance its appeal.

The island is also an attractive choice for expats due to its English-speaking environment and established expat communities, especially in places like Negril and Montego Bay. Good healthcare, wellness retreats, and proximity to the U.S. and Canada make it easier for long-term residents to maintain connections back home while enjoying a healthier lifestyle. While safety concerns exist in some areas, many tourist spots and gated communities are secure, offering peace of mind for those making Jamaica their home.

Best Regions and Cities for Long-Term Living in Jamaica

Jamaica offers several great options for long-term living, each with its own charm. **Montego Bay**, with its blend of urban amenities and stunning beaches, is popular among expats and retirees. It offers a modern lifestyle, luxury resorts, and secure gated communities, making it ideal for those looking for comfort and convenience. **Negril**, known for its laid-back vibe and Seven Mile Beach, is a quieter choice, perfect for those who prefer a slower pace of life in a peaceful, more affordable setting.

Ocho Rios appeals to nature lovers, with its lush landscapes and outdoor attractions like Dunn's River Falls. It's a balance between modern amenities and beautiful scenery. **Kingston**, the capital, is the place for those seeking job opportunities, cultural experiences, and access to top schools and hospitals, though it's more fast-paced. For a quieter, more secluded lifestyle, **Port Antonio** offers a serene environment surrounded by nature, while **Treasure Beach** on the south coast is ideal for those wanting a small, tight-knit community. Other areas like **Runaway Bay** and **St. Ann's Bay** offer a peaceful pace with access to local services, making them great choices for families or retirees.

Living Cost in Jamaica[19]

The cost of living in Jamaica is generally much lower than in the United States, making it an attractive option for expatriates, retirees, and those seeking a more affordable lifestyle. In general terms, you can expect to pay significantly less for most daily expenses, though certain imported goods and services may still be more expensive in Jamaica.

Housing: Rent is one of the biggest savings. A one-bedroom apartment in Jamaica averages about US$473 per month, while in the U.S., the same apartment can cost around US$1,552. Larger homes or luxury rentals will also be significantly cheaper in Jamaica.

Utilities: Monthly utilities (including electricity, water, and internet) in Jamaica are around US$144, compared to US$188 in the U.S. This makes living in Jamaica more budget-friendly, even with the tropical climate.

Food and Dining: Groceries are more affordable in Jamaica, with a monthly grocery bill averaging around US$420 per person. Dining out is also cheaper— a meal at a mid-range restaurant in Jamaica costs about US$8.

---

19   https://www.expatistan.com/cost-of-living/country/jamaica

Transportation: Public transportation is very affordable in Jamaica, with a local ticket costing around US$0.93. Even monthly public transport passes are cheaper.

Healthcare: Healthcare is another area where Jamaica offers savings. A doctor's visit in Jamaica can cost around US$24, compared to US$116 in the U.S., making medical expenses far more affordable.

Housing Options for Long-Term Stays

Finding long-term housing in Jamaica offers a variety of options suited to different preferences and budgets. Popular choices include fully furnished rentals, serviced apartments, and vacation homes, often equipped with essential amenities like kitchens and high-speed internet. Areas like Kingston, Montego Bay, Negril, and Ocho Rios provide diverse rental properties, from cozy studios to luxurious villas, ideal for expatriates and long-term visitors. In more tourist-heavy areas, rentals often come with flexible booking options and easy access to amenities, beaches, and entertainment.

For those seeking a quieter lifestyle, rural areas like Port Antonio and Treasure Beach offer more affordable and secluded options, such as houses and cottages amidst nature. Kingston, the capital, offers both modern apartments and suburban homes with access to the country's top amenities. Gated communities with added security and facilities like pools and gyms are also popular for long-term stays. Overall, rental costs in Jamaica tend to be lower than in Western countries, making it an affordable and attractive destination for long-term living.

You can find long-term rentals in Jamaica through websites like Airbnb, Jamaica Homes, Top Villas, Sotheby's International Realty, and Properstar.

Transportation Options

Long-term visitors to Jamaica have several transportation options to choose from, depending on their needs, location, and budget. For those staying in urban areas or tourist hotspots, **public transportation** offers a cost-effective way to get around. Local buses and minivans, known as "route taxis," are commonly used, though they may not always offer the comfort or reliability of private options. For more flexibility, visitors can also opt for **registered taxis**, which are widely available in most major cities and tourist areas. These taxis are a more convenient choice, especially if you prefer a more direct and comfortable ride.

If you're staying in a more remote area or prefer a bit more independence, **renting a car** is a popular choice. Car rentals are available at major airports like Montego Bay and Kingston, and while driving in Jamaica can be an adjustment due to left-hand driving, the road infrastructure is generally good in urban and tourist areas. Alternatively, some long-term visitors choose to hire a **private driver** or use **ride-sharing** services like Uber in select locations. For those living in or around larger towns and cities, **walking** or **biking** can also be viable options, particularly in safe and well-developed areas. Regardless of the choice, it's important to always consider safety.

Healthcare Options for Long-Term Visitors

Long-term visitors to Jamaica have access to a range of healthcare options, from public hospitals to private medical facilities, depending on their needs and budget. The country offers both public and private healthcare systems, though the quality and cost can vary.

Public healthcare in Jamaica is provided by the government through the Ministry of Health, with major hospitals located in cities like Kingston (e.g., Kingston Public Hospital) and Montego Bay. These facilities offer basic medical services at a much lower cost than private clinics but can sometimes face overcrowding and longer wait times. Public healthcare is generally accessible to all residents, including long-term visitors, but it may not offer the same level of comfort and care as private options.

Private healthcare in Jamaica is often preferred by expatriates and long-term visitors due to its higher standards, shorter wait times, and more personalized care. Private hospitals and clinics, such as the Andrews Memorial Hospital in Kingston or the Montego Bay-based Cornwall Regional Hospital, offer a wide range of services, from routine check-ups to more specialized treatments. While private healthcare is more expensive than public services, it is still generally more affordable than in many Western countries.

For those seeking more comprehensive care or specialized services, many visitors also opt for international health insurance plans that cover medical treatments in Jamaica. Health insurance is recommended to ensure access to the best facilities and avoid high out-of-pocket expenses. Additionally, Jamaica has numerous pharmacies and wellness centers, particularly in larger towns and tourist areas, providing over-the-counter medication and alternative health treatments.

 For tips and quote comparison on international health plans, visit **https://www.pacificprime.com/country/ americas/jamaica-health-insurance/**, or other similar sites.

Language Considerations

Language considerations for long-term foreign visitors in Jamaica are generally straightforward, as English is the official language of the country. This makes it easy for English-speaking visitors, especially those from countries like the United States, Canada, and the UK, to communicate without a language barrier. Whether it's interacting with locals, reading signs, or understanding government documents, English is used in everyday life, including at schools, hospitals, and most businesses.

However, visitors may encounter Jamaican Patois, a creole language that is widely spoken by locals. Patois, a blend of English, African, and other linguistic influences, can be heard in casual conversations, cultural expressions, and music. While it's not typically used in formal settings, understanding some basic phrases or expressions in Patois can help visitors connect with locals on a deeper cultural level and enrich their experience.

For long-term visitors who plan to immerse themselves in local communities or spend time in rural areas, learning a few phrases in Patois can be appreciated by Jamaicans, even though it's not necessary for day-to-day interactions. In tourist areas, hotels, and resorts, English is universally spoken, so communication will generally not be an issue for foreigners.

Long-Term Visas[20]

Long-term visas are permits that allow foreign nationals to stay in a country for an extended period, typically ranging from several months to several years, for purposes like work, study, retirement, or investment. These visas are different from short-term tourist visas, which are generally intended for stays of up to 90 days.

Jamaica has become an increasingly desirable destination for expatriates and long-term visitors. Jamaica offers several options for long-term visas, catering to different needs, whether you're planning to retire, work, invest, or live on the island for an extended period. Here are the main categories:

- **Work Visa:** One of the primary types of long-term visas available is the work visa, which allows foreign nationals to live and work in Jamaica. Applicants seeking a work visa must secure employment from a Jamaican employer willing to sponsor them. This visa grants the holder the right to live and work in Jamaica without the need for a constant renewal of work permits, facilitating smoother employment transitions and residency arrangements.

- **Permanent Residency:** Another option for those looking for an extended stay in Jamaica is permanent residency. Individuals can apply for this status under specific categories such as employment, investment, or family reunification. For instance, foreign nationals who have invested in a business or who are closely related to Jamaican citizens may become eligible for permanent residency. This status allows holders to live and work in Jamaica indefinitely and provides certain rights akin to those enjoyed by Jamaican citizens, though they do not possess full constitutional rights. The approval process

---

20 https://www.pica.gov.jm/immigration/permanent-residence

typically involves an interview and background checks, ensuring that applicants meet the necessary criteria for residency.

- **Student Visa:** For those intending to pursue educational opportunities, a student visa is available for long-term stays. This visa is designed for individuals who have been accepted into a Jamaican educational institution and plan to study full-time. Holders of a student visa may also be permitted to work part-time while studying, although regulations pertaining to employment may vary by institution and course of study. Thus, the student visa offers a dual advantage of educational advancement and professional experience, appealing to international students seeking growth opportunities in their fields.

- **Retirement Visa:** The retirement visa is another avenue for those wishing to reside long-term in Jamaica. Although specific regulations for retirement visas can vary, generally, applicants must demonstrate financial independence and the means to support themselves without employment while living in Jamaica. This type of visa appeals to retirees looking for a peaceful and warm environment to spend their golden years, as Jamaica offers a rich culture and beautiful surroundings conducive to relaxation and leisure.

- **Family Reunification Visa:** Lastly, the family reunification visa allows foreign nationals to reside in Jamaica based on familial connections to Jamaican citizens or permanent residents. This visa category is particularly relevant for spouses, children, and dependent relatives. Applicants must submit proof of their relationship to their Jamaican family members, such as marriage certificates or birth certificates, to qualify. This category reinforces the importance of family ties in immigration processes and facilitates the unity of families separated by international borders.

Residency Requirements for Foreigners

Foreigners seeking to live long-term in Jamaica must meet specific residency requirements based on the type of visa they're applying for. For temporary residency, foreigners can apply for work, student, or retirement visas, each with different criteria. Work visas require a job offer from a Jamaican employer, while student visas need proof of enrollment in a recognized educational institution. Retirees aged 55 or older can apply for a retirement visa by showing proof of sufficient financial resources to support themselves without working.

For permanent residency, foreigners must typically live in Jamaica for at least five years on a temporary visa. Investors who make significant contributions to the Jamaican economy can apply for permanent residency, as can individuals married to Jamaican citizens or with Jamaican family members. Applicants must demonstrate financial stability, good health, and good conduct. After holding permanent residency for five years, individuals may be eligible for Jamaican citizenship. Each visa type has specific documentation requirements and a defined application process through the Jamaican Immigration Service. For more information, please visit Passport, Immigration and Citizenship Agency at https://www.pica.gov.jm/.

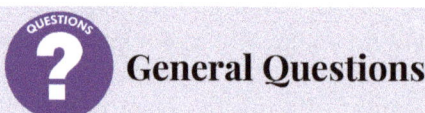 **General Questions**

1. *If I want to stay in Jamaica long-term and work, should I apply for a work permit before arriving in Jamaica?* Yes. Jamaica has a two-tier system for work permits. U.S. citizens and nationals from other countries must secure a work permit prior to entering Jamaica if they wish to work. On the other hand, citizens from Commonwealth countries can enter Jamaica on a tourist visa and apply for a work permit once they are in the country.

2. ***I am American. Can I retire to Jamaica?*** Yes. As an American, you can stay in Jamaica for up to six months without a visa. To stay longer, you will need to apply for residency status. As part of your application, you will need your passport, evidence you can financially support yourself without working, and a completed application form, which you can find at the Jamaican consulate.

3. ***What happens if I overstay my visa in Jamaica?*** If you overstay your visa in Jamaica, you may face fines, deportation, and a ban from re-entering the country for a period of time. The fines can vary depending on how long you've overstayed, and immigration officers will assess your case. It's important to leave the country before your visa expires or to apply for an extension if you plan to stay longer.

4. ***What income requirements are there for a long-stay visa in Jamaica?*** Regarding income requirements for a long-stay visa in Jamaica, these can vary depending on the type of visa you are applying for (e.g., a retirement visa, work visa, or visitor visa). Generally, you will need to demonstrate proof of sufficient financial means to support yourself during your stay. For example, retirees may need to show a steady monthly income or savings to cover living expenses. Specific amounts can be obtained by contacting the Jamaican immigration office or consulting their official guidelines.

 ## Law of the Land Hypothetical

HYPOTHETICAL: *Charles has had a wonderful time in Jamaica during his two-week vacation and has decided to stay for a year and work. Will he need to return to his home country to obtain the necessary paperwork, or can he apply for it while staying in Jamaica?*

ANSWER: *Charles, as a citizen of a non-Commonwealth country, will likely need to apply for the necessary work permit before entering Jamaica, as he has already overstayed the duration of his initial stay. For non-Commonwealth nationals, work permits must typically be obtained before arrival in Jamaica. However, he may be able to apply for an extension or change his visa status while in the country, depending on the circumstances, though this process can be more complicated than applying from abroad. It's advisable for Charles to consult with the Jamaican immigration authorities or a legal expert to determine the best course of action.*

 **Law of the Land True Story**

Omar Cogle, a U.S. citizen, was ordered deported from Jamaica after overstaying his visa. Cogle, who had been sent to Jamaica as a minor, was arrested at the age of 22 for violating the Immigration Act. Despite being granted six months to stay in the country, he remained past his allowed time. The judge issued a deportation order, directing Cogle's mother to quickly arrange his travel. He was held in custody until his departure was confirmed.

CIVIL LITIGATION

CIVIL LITIGATION

Overview

Civil litigation provides a mechanism for resolving disputes, ensuring that travelers have a way to seek justice if legal issues arise while visiting another country. It helps them understand their rights and obligations under local laws, which may differ from those in their home country. The civil litigation system offers a formal process for addressing conflicts, such as contract disputes or personal injury claims, and can deter unfair practices by encouraging businesses to comply with legal standards. It also allows individuals to seek financial recourse for damages or losses and helps protect them from potential exploitation by local entities. Overall, understanding civil litigation enhances a visitor's experience and safety while traveling.

Personal Injury Claims and Compensation Law[21]

Jamaica, known for its beautiful landscapes and vibrant culture, is a popular destination for tourists, but accidents resulting in personal injury can create legal challenges for visitors. Foreign tourists who suffer injuries on the island need to understand Jamaica's personal injury claims process and compensation laws. These laws cover various

---

21 https://www.hg.org/legal-articles/foreigners-personal-injury-law-and-compensation-in-jamaica-understanding-your-case-28610

incidents, such as motor vehicle accidents, slip and fall accidents, and injuries caused by negligence. Victims can seek compensation for medical expenses, pain and suffering, lost wages, and other related damages. However, foreign visitors must navigate Jamaica's legal system, which, while similar to the U.S. and Canada in its common law principles, has its own procedural nuances.

Foreign visitors in Jamaica have the right to pursue personal injury claims, but they must adhere to specific timelines, typically within two years from the date of the accident. It's important to consult with local legal experts, as liability standards and available compensation may differ from those in the visitor's home country. Many personal injury claims in Jamaica are handled on a contingency fee basis, meaning visitors pay legal fees only if compensation is awarded. Insurance, particularly travel insurance that covers medical expenses and personal injury, is highly recommended for tourists. Claims are typically processed through either the Resident Magistrate Court or the Supreme Court, depending on the claim's size, and local attorneys are essential for navigating the legal procedures and ensuring a favorable outcome.

To pursue a personal injury claim in Jamaica, follow these key steps:

1. **Seek Medical Attention:** Immediately visit a doctor or hospital to document your injuries, which is essential for your claim.

2. **Gather Evidence:** Collect evidence, including photos of the accident scene, witness contact details, accident reports, and records of your medical expenses and financial losses.

3. **Contact a Local Attorney:** Hire an experienced local attorney who can guide you through Jamaica's legal system, ensuring all documents are correctly filed and deadlines met.

4. **File the Claim:** Your attorney will prepare and submit a letter of claim to the responsible party. If no settlement is reached, the case will be filed in the appropriate court, depending on the claim's value.

5. **Statute of Limitations:** Personal injury claims must generally be filed within three years from the date of the injury. Failing to do so may result in losing the right to claim compensation.

How to File a Civil Claim

Filing a civil claim in Jamaica involves understanding the local legal framework, which is based on common law influenced by British traditions. Civil claims in Jamaica can cover a wide range of issues, such as negligence, contracts, property disputes, and family law matters. To initiate a claim, individuals must first establish the legal basis for their case and determine the appropriate type of relief. This process requires careful attention to statutory guidelines and an understanding of the procedures involved.

When filing a civil claim in Jamaica, the process begins by determining which court has jurisdiction over your case. If it's a relatively small claim, valued under J$1 million, it will typically be handled by the Resident Magistrate's Court. More complex or higher-value cases are directed to the Supreme Court. Once you've identified the appropriate court, the next step is to prepare your statement of claim. This document outlines the facts of your case, the legal grounds for your claim, and the relief you're seeking.

After the statement is ready, you file it with the court and pay the necessary filing fee. The court will then issue a claim form, which must be served to the defendant. This is known as the "service of process," and it notifies the defendant of the legal action against them. The defendant typically has 14 days to respond by filing a defense. Once both sides have presented their claims and defenses, the case proceeds to trial unless a settlement is reached beforehand. If either party is dissatisfied with the court's decision, they have the right to appeal to a higher court. Given the complexities involved, it's highly recommended to consult with a local attorney who can guide you through the process and ensure that all legal requirements are met.

Fees and Deadlines[22]

Navigating civil claims in Jamaica requires understanding the associated fees and deadlines. Fees vary depending on the type of claim, the court

---

22 https://supremecourt.gov.jm/content/fees-and-costs

involved, and services required, such as expert witnesses or attorney's fees. Filing fees typically range from J$5,000, with additional costs for professional services and legal representation. As claims progress, costs can include witness fees, document preparation, and court appearances, making it essential for claimants to budget effectively.

Deadlines play a crucial role in civil claims, with most cases needing to be filed within three years of the incident. Defendants must respond within 42 days, or they risk a default judgment. Appeals also have strict time limits, usually between 14 and 42 days. Failure to meet this deadline can result in a default judgment. Appeals also have time limits, generally ranging from 14 to 42 days depending on the case specifics.

Service of Documents

In Jamaica, the legal framework surrounding the service of documents is outlined primarily in the Civil Procedure Rules (CPR) and the Limitation of Actions Act. The rules establish the necessity for all parties to be properly notified of legal proceedings initiated against them. Specifically, the CPR stipulates the methods of service permitted and the requirements that must be met to ensure that service is valid. It is crucial for the serving party to comply with these regulations to avoid potential legal repercussions and ensure that the court has jurisdiction over the matter.

Methods of Service

There are various methods available for serving documents in Jamaica, each designated for specific situations. The most common methods include:

- **Personal Service:** This method involves delivering the document directly to the individual intended to receive it. Personal service is the most straightforward and reliable form of service as it ensures that the recipient is aware of the legal action.
- **Service by Mail:** This method may be employed if the recipient's address is known. However, it is essential that service by mail complies

with local rules, which may require confirmation of receipt by the recipient.

- **Service by a Process Server:** Employing a registered process server to deliver legal documents is widely considered the best practice, as they are proficient in adhering to legal requirements while ensuring proper service. Private process servers significantly hasten the service process and ensure compliance with local laws.

- **Service by Publication:** If the whereabouts of the defendant are unknown or when personal service cannot be effectuated despite reasonable effort, courts may grant permission to serve by publication. This requires obtaining a court order allowing the serving party to publish a notice in a recognized newspaper.

- **Letters Rogatory:** This formal request is utilized when services involve cross-border document serving, directing a foreign court to assist in serving a claim or pleadings. This method is usually more time-consuming and cumbersome, making it less favorable than local service methods.

Responsible Parties

In the legal process, ensuring proper service of documents is the responsibility of the party initiating the action. This typically falls to the claimant or plaintiff, who is tasked with proving that the defendant has been adequately notified of the proceedings. To fulfill this responsibility, the claimant may enlist the help of process servers—authorized individuals or agencies specializing in delivering legal documents on their behalf. In some cases, court officials may also serve documents, either as part of their official duties or upon specific request, depending on the type of case.

Steps in the Service of Documents

The service of documents in Jamaica involves several critical steps:

- **Preparation of Documents:** Before service can occur, necessary documents, such as the claim form and statement of claim, must be accurately prepared and finalized.

- **Selection of Service Method:** The claimant must decide on the most appropriate method of service based on the specific circumstances of the case.

- **Execution of Service:** The selected method is then executed, whether through personal delivery, mail, or a process server. This step must be conducted carefully to ensure compliance with all legal requirements.

- **Documentation of Service:** Following service, the process server (or the individual who served the documents) is responsible for completing a Proof of Service document, typically an affidavit, detailing the service process. This must include information such as who was served, how, and when.

- **Filing the Proof of Service:** The proof of service must be filed with the court as evidence that the service has been properly executed. This document is crucial for the case to proceed, as it verifies that due process has been observed.

Proof of Service

Proof of service is an essential component of the legal process in Jamaica. It is typically provided in the form of an affidavit of service, which is a sworn declaration confirming how, when, and upon whom the legal documents were served. This proof enables the court to ascertain that the defendant received notice of the proceedings, which is a critical factor for the court's jurisdiction. Failing to provide adequate proof of service can lead to significant delays and potential dismissal of the claim, thereby hampering the plaintiff's chances of success in court.

Statute of Limitations

In Jamaica, the legal framework governing civil claims stipulates specific time limits, known as statutes of limitations, within which parties must initiate legal action. These time limits vary depending on the type of claim being filed and are designed to promote timely resolution of disputes while protecting parties from prolonged uncertainty.

Tort Claims

One of the most common types of civil suits pertains to tort actions. In Jamaica the statute of limitations for actions in tort is set at **six years** from the date on which the cause of action arose. This includes claims for negligence, assault, and defamation, among others. The injured party must initiate the claim within this six-year window; failing to do so typically results in the claim being barred and unable to proceed in court.[23]

Breach of Contract Claims

For claims involving breach of contract, the statute of limitations is also **six years**. The clock for this limitation begins when the breach occurs, meaning that claimants must act swiftly upon discovering the breach to enforce their rights. Whether the breach involves non-performance or delayed performance, parties seeking to recover damages must adhere to this timeline, or they risk losing the opportunity to pursue legal recourse.

Claims for Defamation

Defamation claims in Jamaica carry a shorter statute of limitations. According to the Defamation Act, actions for defamation must be brought within **two years** from the date of first publication. This strict timeline reflects the importance of timely resolution in cases where a party's reputation is at stake. Therefore, individuals who believe they have been defamed must act quickly to preserve their rights and seek remediation.

Wrongful Death Claims

In instances of wrongful death, claims must be made within **three years** after the date of death. This timeframe applies to claims filed under the Fatal Accidents Act for the benefit of dependents of the deceased person.

---

23 https://jamaica-gleaner.com/article/flair/20190624/
    laws-eve-time-limits-civil-proceedings

If the case involves claims made for the deceased's estate, the six-year limitation applies, further emphasizing the importance of understanding the specifics of the claim being pursued.[24]

Matrimonial Property Claims

Under the Property (Rights of Spouses) Act, actions concerning matrimonial property must be initiated within **twelve months** following the dissolution of marriage, termination of cohabitation, or separation. This relatively short timeframe compels spouses to act promptly in asserting their rights regarding property division, emphasizing the urgent nature of these claims in the context of family law.

Getting Married in Jamaica

Jamaica is a popular destination for couples seeking to tie the knot, particularly for foreigners wishing to embrace the island's breathtaking scenery and vibrant culture. However, navigating the legal requirements for marriage in Jamaica requires understanding the necessary documentation, processes involved, associated fees, and recognition of the marriage internationally.

Foreign nationals intending to marry in Jamaica are required to present specific documents to comply with local laws. The essential documents include:

- **Proof of Citizenship:** A certified copy of the birth certificate, which must include the father's name

- **Parental Consent:** If any party is under 18 years of age, written parental consent from both parents is mandatory, along with proof of their identity

- **Proof of Divorce or Death:** If applicable, a certified copy of the original divorce decree must be provided for those who have previously

---

24 https://jamaica-gleaner.com/article/flair/20190624/
laws-eve-time-limits-civil-proceedings#

been married. For widows or widowers, a certified copy of the deceased spouse's death certificate is required.

- **Translated Documentation:** Any documents not in English must be translated by an official translator and notarized
- **A government-issued photo ID or passport** may also be required to verify identity.

Obtaining a marriage license in Jamaica is a relatively simple process. There are no residency requirements for foreign couples; couples must apply at the Ministry of Justice or through a designated Marriage Officer, submitting an application form and the required documents. The marriage license fee is approximately J$4,000 (around US$25 to US$35), and the application is usually processed on the same day. Foreigners can marry just 24 hours after applying, provided all necessary documents are in order, though some venues may require additional time. Beyond the marriage license fee, couples should anticipate additional costs. The fees for a Marriage Officer range from US$50 to US$250, depending on the individual's service and experience. Additional expenses for the wedding ceremony, such as venue, floral arrangements, and photography, should also be factored into the overall budget.[25]

Marriages conducted in Jamaica are generally recognized internationally, provided they comply with all legal requirements set forth by Jamaican law. After the wedding, couples will receive a Marriage Register, which serves as proof of marriage, although they will also need to obtain a certified copy of the marriage certificate for legal matters. If the couple's country of origin requires additional legalization processes, they must consult their local embassy or consulate in Jamaica to authenticate the marriage certificate, ensuring it meets the legal standards in their home country.

---

25 http://www.jhcuk.org/visitors/getting-married-in-jamaica

 **Law of the Land True Story**

On February 19, 2021, after a trial, the court ruled in favor of Mrs. Trudy-Anne Silent-Hyatt in her negligence claim against Mr. Rohan Marley and Mr. Jason Walters. The claim stemmed from a motor vehicle accident on April 15, 2016, when Mr. Walters, driving a motor truck owned by Mr. Marley, rear-ended Mrs. Silent-Hyatt's car as they were traveling along Half Way Tree Road in Saint Andrew. Mrs. Silent-Hyatt was awarded J$5,000,000 (US$32,247.26) for general damages related to pain, suffering, and loss of amenities, along with J$218,094.36 (US$1,406.59) for special damages, and J$900,000 (US$5,804.51) for post-traumatic stress disorder. On appeal, the judgment was upheld, and an additional US$75,800.00 was granted for future medical care.

OTHER THINGS TO KNOW

- Tourists and Street Hustling
- Safety Concerns and Practical Tips
- In the Event of Death

OTHER THINGS TO KNOW

Tourists and Street Hustling

Street hustling in Jamaica, although not always criminal, remains a persistent issue, particularly in areas frequented by tourists. The practice has long been acknowledged by the government, which has made efforts to address it, but it continues to affect many visitors. Hustling can take many forms, from the harmless and persistent street vendor offering souvenirs, to more intrusive encounters involving the sale of illegal items such as marijuana or unlicensed services like unofficial tour guiding and hair braiding. Some tourists, particularly women, may also face sexual harassment in the form of suggestive comments or unsolicited attention.

In the past, the problem of street hustling was more widespread, with around 60 percent of tourists reporting harassment in the mid-1990s. While this figure has dropped to about one in three visitors, the issue persists, especially in high-traffic areas such as Montego Bay, Negril, Ocho Rios, and Kingston. In these places, it's common for tourists to be approached by individuals attempting to sell everything from handcrafted jewelry and T-shirts to fake "genuine Jamaican" goods. Hustlers often employ a variety of techniques to draw tourists in, starting with friendly conversation or a flattering compliment before pushing a product or service, sometimes at inflated prices.

The goods and services on offer range widely. Often, tourists are approached with souvenir items like wood carvings, artwork, or clothing, many of which are advertised as "authentic" or rare. In some cases, hustlers attempt to sell marijuana, which remains illegal for tourists despite the decriminalization of small amounts for personal use by locals. Another common hustle involves hair braiding or beauty services, especially on beaches where visitors may be offered "free" or heavily discounted services, only to find themselves charged exorbitantly afterward. Unofficial tour guides also frequently approach tourists, promising unique experiences and lower rates than licensed guides, but often delivering subpar service or overcharging after the fact. There are also instances where hustlers offer illegal transportation services, posing as legitimate taxi drivers.

In addition to these scams, tourists may encounter more deceptive practices such as fake tours or overcharging. It's not unusual for a hustler to offer a "free" tour of an attraction, only to demand payment at the end or claim that the tourist agreed to a fee upfront. Some hustlers also employ tactics like handing tourists' items, such as flowers or small trinkets, with the expectation that the tourist will feel obligated to pay for them. Once a payment is requested, refusal often leads to verbal aggression or harassment.

The Jamaican government and local authorities have made strides in addressing street hustling. They've introduced designated vending zones in certain tourist areas where street vendors can legally operate, though many hustlers ignore these boundaries and continue to ply their trade in unregulated spaces. Enforcement can be inconsistent, with some hustlers managing to evade penalties by moving quickly or using other tactics to avoid detection. Occasionally, police will conduct raids to remove unauthorized vendors or arrest individuals for selling illegal items, but tourists often report a sense of uneven enforcement, with some areas being more heavily patrolled than others.

Despite these efforts, the problem persists, and visitors need to stay vigilant. Authorities continue to run public awareness campaigns to educate tourists about street hustling and advise them to remain cautious when approached by anyone offering unsolicited goods or services. Tourists are encouraged to avoid engaging in illegal activities, such as purchasing marijuana or accepting unlicensed services, and to stick to licensed tour guides and transportation services. It's also wise for tourists to be informed about the going rates for goods and services in popular tourist areas, so they can quickly spot any overcharging attempts. In cases where harassment or scams occur, tourists are urged to report the incident to local authorities or their hotel staff.

While street hustling is an unfortunate aspect of the tourist experience in Jamaica, most visitors can successfully navigate it with a firm, respectful approach. Being aware of the common hustles, scams, and the areas most affected by them can help tourists protect themselves and avoid falling victim to deceitful practices. By maintaining a polite but firm demeanor and avoiding the temptation to engage in illegal activities, visitors can enjoy their time in Jamaica without undue harassment.

Safety Concerns and Practical Tips

Interacting with street hustlers in Jamaica can present several safety risks, from financial loss to physical harm. The main safety concerns for visitors in Jamaica related to street hustling include the risk of being overcharged for goods or services, falling victim to scams, or encountering aggressive or threatening behavior. These interactions can sometimes escalate, putting visitors at risk of being scammed, robbed, or caught in unsafe situations. Staying alert and cautious is crucial to avoiding such risks.

To protect themselves, tourists should familiarize themselves with local pricing and always confirm costs before agreeing to any service. It's best to avoid engaging with hustlers for long periods and to politely decline offers. Carrying limited cash and using official tour operators or taxis can also reduce risks. Tourists should stay aware of their surroundings, avoid displaying valuables, and retreat to hotels or public places if feeling threatened.

There are several resources available for tourists who experience harassment or scams in Jamaica. The Ministry of Tourism has established a

"Tourism Alert" hotline, where tourists can report any incidents involving street hustling, harassment, or scams: (876) 920-4926-30.

Additionally, many hotels have dedicated guest services or security teams who can assist in handling harassment or unsafe situations. In cases of more serious crimes, tourists can report incidents to the local police. While the police response can vary depending on the area, they are required to investigate any reports of crime or harassment.

Tourists can also use the Jamaica Tourist Board's official website to find helpful safety information, local resources, and tips for reporting issues during their stay. Social media platforms and travel forums like TripAdvisor or Lonely Planet's Thorn Tree forum can be helpful places for tourists to share experiences and receive advice from fellow travelers. These platforms often provide real-time updates on areas to avoid and safety tips for specific locations.

In the Event of Death

Experiencing the death of a loved one while traveling can be one of the most distressing situations a person can face. The emotional turmoil is compounded by the logistics and legalities involved in handling the remains, informing authorities, and arranging repatriation if necessary.

The first and most crucial action after the death of a traveler is to confirm the situation by seeking immediate medical assistance. If the individual dies after failing to respond, call emergency services at **119** in Jamaica or have a local hotel staff member assist in contacting authorities. Once medical personnel arrive, they will confirm the death, issue a medical certificate, and take necessary legal actions without further delay.

After the official confirmation of death, you must notify the local authorities. This can be done by contacting the nearest police station, which is required to document the incident and issue a report. This report is essential for further processes related to handling the remains and repatriation.

Once local authorities are informed and the necessary documents are procured, you must consider how to handle the remains. Funeral directors or local funeral homes are typically equipped to prepare the body for further actions, including burial or repatriation. It is advisable to engage the services of a reputable funeral home that can guide you through the available options and procedures. A local funeral home in Jamaica will assist with preparing the body, including embalming if required, and ensuring compliance with local and international regulations for transportation. They will also help obtain essential documentation, such as the death certificate, which is crucial for repatriation and legal purposes. If there are delays, the funeral home may arrange for cold storage to preserve the remains until all procedures are complete.

In the event of repatriation, the process involves several critical steps. First, you must consult with a licensed funeral director experienced in international repatriation, who will guide you through the necessary legalities and paperwork. Key documents required for repatriation include an official **death certificate**, an **embalming certificate**, and a **transit permit** from the local health department. The funeral home will coordinate transportation, which may involve special arrangements with airlines for a suitable container for the remains. It's also important to inform your home country's embassy or consulate about the death, as they can assist with additional documentation and support throughout the process.

CHAPTER 26
QUICK REFERENCE GUIDE

- Quick Chapter References to Important Topics

QUICK REFERENCE GUIDE

Crime in Jamaica

Are there particular areas I should avoid as a tourist?

While Jamaica is a popular and vibrant tourist destination, there are certain areas where visitors should exercise extra caution. **Kingston**, particularly in neighborhoods like Trench Town and Tivoli Gardens, has higher crime rates, as do some parts of **Montego Bay** and **Ocho Rios** outside tourist hubs. Negril's popular Seven Mile Beach is safe, but less frequented areas may pose risks, especially at night. Remote rural regions can also be isolated and lack infrastructure, making them less secure for tourists. To stay safe, stick to well-populated areas, use reputable transportation, avoid displaying valuables, and seek local advice on where to go. *For more details, see Chapter 3.*

Drug Offenses

Is the possession of marijuana legal?

In Jamaica, the possession of marijuana is **partially legal**. Since 2015, the possession of small amounts of marijuana (up to 2 ounces) for personal use has been decriminalized, meaning it is not treated as a criminal offense but as a civil one, with a fine of J$500 (approximately US$3) if caught. Additionally, it is legal for religious use (such as for Rastafarians) and for medical purposes, given that a license is obtained. However, public smoking or consumption of marijuana is prohibited, and marijuana use should still be done discreetly and in private spaces.

Is the possession of cocaine legal?

The possession of cocaine remains **illegal** in Jamaica. Cocaine is classified as a controlled substance, and its possession, trafficking, or distribution is considered a serious criminal offense. Those caught with cocaine can face severe legal penalties, including lengthy prison sentences. *For more details, see Chapter 4.*

Alcohol-Related Offenses

What is the legal drinking age?

The legal drinking age in Jamaica is **18 years old.** This applies to the purchase and consumption of alcoholic beverages in public places such as bars, clubs, and restaurants.

What is the legal blood alcohol limit to drive?

In Jamaica, the legal blood alcohol concentration (BAC) limit for drivers is **0.08%.** This is the same limit typically observed in many countries for private vehicle drivers. If a driver exceeds this limit, they may face penalties such as fines, license suspension, or even arrest. It's important to note that penalties can be stricter for commercial drivers. *For more details, see Chapter 5.*

Firearm & Ammunition Offenses

Can I possess a gun?

It is **illegal** for civilians to possess firearms in Jamaica without a valid license. Firearm licenses are issued by the Firearm Licensing Authority (FLA), but obtaining one is a lengthy and strict process, typically granted only to those who can demonstrate a legitimate need (such as for personal protection, security services, or hunting) and pass background checks. Unauthorized possession of a firearm can result in severe penalties, including imprisonment.

Can I possess ammunition?

The possession of ammunition without the proper licensing is also illegal. This includes carrying or storing ammunition without a firearm license. Violating ammunition laws can lead to criminal charges, including significant fines and imprisonment. *For more details, see Chapter 6.*

Prostitution

Is prostitution legal?

Prostitution is **not legal** in Jamaica. While the act of selling sex is not explicitly prohibited, soliciting sex (either by the seller or the buyer) is illegal and can lead to arrest. The Jamaican government has laws against public solicitation, brothel-keeping, and other activities related to the prostitution industry. Despite this, the sex trade does exist in certain areas, often operating covertly. *For more details, see Chapter 7.*

LGBTQ

Is homosexuality legal?

Homosexuality is technically legal in Jamaica, but there are significant legal and cultural challenges. Same-sex sexual activity is criminalized under the buggery laws (Section 76 of the Offenses Against the Person Act), which prohibits anal sex between men. However, these laws are rarely enforced, and there is no law that explicitly bans homosexuality itself. Despite this, the legal environment remains difficult for LGBTQ+ individuals due to persistent societal stigmas and discrimination.

Are same sex public displays of affection legal?

There is no specific law in Jamaica that criminalizes same-sex public displays of affection (PDA). However, due to the conservative nature of Jamaican society, public expressions of same-sex affection are generally not accepted and could result in social stigma or harassment. While such displays are not illegal, LGBTQ+ individuals may face hostility or violence, especially in public or rural areas where traditional values are more strongly upheld. Many LGBTQ+ people in Jamaica, including tourists, exercise discretion and caution when it comes to public behavior. *For more details, see Chapter 8.*

Arrested in Jamaica

Would I be entitled to bail if I'm arrested?

Yes, you may be entitled to bail if you are arrested in Jamaica, though it depends on the offense. For less serious crimes, bail is typically granted. However, for more serious offenses such as violent crimes, bail can be denied or granted with stricter conditions. The decision to grant bail is made by a judge or magistrate based on factors like the severity of the crime and the likelihood of the person fleeing or interfering with the case.

Will a lawyer be provided to me if I cannot afford one?

Yes, if you cannot afford a lawyer in Jamaica, one will be provided to you through the Legal Aid Council. The council provides free legal representation to individuals who meet financial eligibility criteria, especially in criminal cases. If you cannot afford a lawyer, you should inform the court or authorities, and they will arrange for a legal aid lawyer to represent you. *For more details, see Chapter 10.*

Helping a Friend or Relative Imprisoned in Jamaica

Can I send money to a friend or relative imprisoned in Jamaica?

You can send money to a friend or family member imprisoned in Jamaica. There are several ways to send money, including through money transfer services like Western Union or MoneyGram, or by depositing funds into the inmate's prison account directly. It's important to check with the specific correctional facility for the procedures and accepted methods, as the regulations can vary between institutions.

Can I remain in Jamaica upon release from prison or jail after my sentence is complete?

> Whether you can remain in Jamaica after serving your sentence depends on your immigration status. If you are a foreign national, you would need to have a valid visa or residence status to remain in the country after your release. If you do not have the necessary legal documentation, you may be required to leave Jamaica. However, in some cases, immigration authorities may allow an extension or a change of status depending on individual circumstances. *For more details, see Chapter 12.*

Crime Victim Assistance

Can a victim of a crime be legally compensated?

> **Yes**, victims of crime in Jamaica can be legally compensated through the Jamaica Victim Support Program (VSP), which is a government initiative aimed at assisting victims of violent crimes. While the compensation is not always automatic, victims can apply for financial assistance for medical treatment, funeral expenses, and other related costs. The VSP also provides emotional support and guidance throughout the legal process. Additionally, victims may seek compensation through the courts if the offender is found guilty and ordered to pay restitution, though this may not always result in full reimbursement.

Does the Jamaican government offer assistance for family members of homicide victims?

> The Jamaican government offers assistance to family members of homicide victims through the Victim Support Program (VSP). The program provides emotional support, counseling, and guidance to help families cope with their loss. Financial assistance may also be available to cover funeral expenses and related costs. In addition, families can access legal support to help navigate the justice system, ensuring they receive appropriate compensation and justice. *For more details, see Chapter 14.*

U.S. Consulate Assistance

Are there any limitations to the consulate assistance I can receive while in Jamaica?

Yes, consular assistance in Jamaica has limits. The embassy can help with legal issues, passport replacement, and emergencies, but cannot intervene in legal disputes, provide financial aid, or offer legal representation. Their role is to protect your rights and assist with navigating local systems, not solve personal problems. *For more details, please see Chapter 14.*

Police

Is there an official police force?

Jamaica has an official police force known as the **Jamaica Constabulary Force (JCF)**. The JCF is responsible for maintaining law and order, preventing and investigating crimes, and ensuring the safety and security of the public across the island. It is one of the primary law enforcement agencies in Jamaica and operates under the Ministry of National Security.

What is the contact number for a police emergency in Jamaica?

The emergency number for police assistance in Jamaica is 119. This number connects you directly to the Jamaica Constabulary Force for emergency response, whether it involves criminal activity, accidents, or other law enforcement issues. It is the equivalent of 911 in many other countries. *For more details, see Chapter 15.*

How to Get Legal Help in Jamaica

Is there a resource in Jamaica to find legal representation?

A good resource to find legal representation is the Jamaican Bar Association, that can be reached at 876-967-1528 and though their website **jambar.org**.

The U.S. Embassy in Kingston, located at 142 Old Hope Road, can provide a list of local attorneys who can represent U.S. citizens in

Jamaica, accessible at **common.usembassy.gov/wp-content/up-loads/sites/88/2022/11/New-Attorney-List-Ja.pdf.**

Is there free legal representation assistance?

Yes, free legal representation is available in Jamaica through the Legal Aid Council, which provides assistance to individuals who cannot afford a lawyer. Eligible individuals, based on financial need and the nature of their case, can receive legal aid for criminal, civil, or family matters. Law schools and nonprofit organizations may also offer pro bono services. *For more details, see Chapter 16.*

Foreign Embassies in Jamaica

Are there foreign embassies in Jamaica?

There are many foreign embassies in Jamaica. Many countries, including the United States, Canada, the United Kingdom, and several others, have diplomatic missions in Kingston, Jamaica.

Is there a website to locate embassies in Jamaica?

To locate embassies in Jamaica, you can visit the Ministry of Foreign Affairs and Foreign Trade of Jamaica's official website or consult embassy directories online for specific embassy contact details and locations. *For more details, see Chapter 16.*

Medical Facilities & Hospitals

Is there a number I can call for an ambulance and for fire emergencies?

In Jamaica, the emergency number for ambulance services is 110, and for fire emergencies, it is 811.

If I am injured while on vacation in Jamaica, are there hospitals that are recommended for tourists?

In Jamaica, several hospitals cater to tourists seeking medical care. In Kingston, Kingston Public Hospital is the largest public facility, while University Hospital of the West Indies (UHWI) is a well-regarded teaching hospital. In western Jamaica, Cornwall Regional

Hospital in Montego Bay serves as the primary public hospital, with Sandy Bay Clinic offering private healthcare options. For more personalized services, private hospitals like Medical Associates Hospital in Kingston and SurgiMed in Montego Bay are also available. *For more details, see Chapter 17.*

Driving in Jamaica

Which side of the road do I drive on?

In Jamaica, you drive on the left side of the road.

Can I use my driver's license from my home country to drive in Jamaica?

You can use your driver's license from your home country to drive in Jamaica, as long as it's in English or accompanied by a translation. However, it's often recommended to have an International Driving Permit (IDP) as an additional form of identification.

How old do I need to be to rent a car?

To rent a car in Jamaica, you generally need to be at least **21 years old**, though some rental agencies may require you to be 25 or older. Drivers under 25 may also face additional fees. *For more details, see Chapter 18.*

Nude Beaches & Clothing-Optional Resorts

Is public nudity legal on the beaches?

No, public nudity is not legal on the beaches in Jamaica. Public nudity is generally prohibited in public places, including beaches, unless you're in a designated clothing-optional resort or private property where it's allowed. Most popular beaches and resorts maintain a standard of modesty, so it's advisable to wear appropriate swimwear. *For more details, see Chapter 19.*

Tourist Taxation

Is there a room tax in Jamaica?

Yes, the Jamaican government imposes a room tax on accommodations. The tax rate varies depending on the type of property, but it generally ranges from J$100 to J$400 per night for each guest, depending on the classification of the hotel or accommodation.

Is there any fee associated with leaving Jamaica?

For leaving Jamaica, there is no specific fee for departing the country itself. However, visitors may be required to pay a departure tax, which is often included in the cost of your airline ticket. In some cases, if not included, the tax can be paid at the airport before departure. The standard departure tax is around J$1,000 for Jamaican citizens and residents, and J$2,000 for non-residents. *For more details, see Chapter 22.*

Long-Term Stays

Do I need to return to my home country to apply for a work permit in Jamaica?

As an American, you do not need to return to your home country to apply for a work permit in Jamaica. You can apply for a work permit while in Jamaica if you are already in the country under a tourist visa. However, you will need to obtain a job offer from a Jamaican employer who will submit the work permit application on your behalf to the Jamaica Ministry of Labour and Social Security.

As an American, how long can I stay in Jamaica without a visa?

As a U.S. citizen, you can stay in Jamaica for up to 90 days without a visa for tourism purposes. If you wish to stay longer or engage in activities like work or study, you will need to apply for the appropriate visa or extension before your initial stay expires. *For more details, see Chapter 23.*

In the Event of Death

What documents would an embassy need regarding the death of a tourist?

When a tourist dies in Jamaica, the embassy typically requires several key documents to assist with repatriation and legal processes. These include the official death certificate, the deceased's passport, an embalming certificate, and a transit permit confirming the body's fitness for transport. Additionally, a medical report (if applicable) and the contact information of the deceased's next of kin or family members are needed. The embassy provides support in navigating these steps and coordinating the repatriation process. *For more details, see Chapter 25.*

EMERGENCY/IMPORTANT CONTACT NUMBERS IN JAMAICA

 Please consider putting some of these numbers in your phone prior to traveling to Jamaica.

EMERGENCY NUMBERS:

POLICE: 119

FIRE: 110

AMBULANCE: 110

If you need assistance in the city of Kingston, you can reach the police hotline 24 hours a day at 1-876-927-9910 or 1-876-927-7681 or 1-876-927-7778.

Other general emergency numbers

HURRICANE UPDATE: 116

GENERAL INFORMATION: 114

LIFELINE MEDICAL RESPONSE: 1-876-974-6404

JAMAICA RED CROSS: 1-876-984-7860

AIR-SEA RESCUE: 119

AIR AMBULANCE:
International: 1-832-900-9000
Domestic: 1-800-424-9000

COAST GUARD: 1-876-967-8031/8223/8190-3

STOLEN MOTOR VEHICLE: 119 / 1-876-922-3771 OR 1-876-927-7681-2

THE LEGAL AID COUNCIL
Telephone: 1-876-948-6999

THE JAMAICAN BAR ASSOCIATION
Telephone: 1-876-967-3394
Email: jambarassoc@gmail.com

USEFUL JAMAICAN PATOIS PHRASES

GREETINGS

HI/HELLO – Wah gwaan / Hail up

GOOD MORNING – Mornin'

GOOD AFTERNOON – Good aftanoon

GOOD NIGHT – Good night

GOODBYE – Likkle more / Mi gone

MAGIC WORDS

PLEASE – Mi a beg yuh / Please

THANK YOU – Tanks / Nuff respect

YOU'RE WELCOME – Nuh wah / Yuh welcome

CHEERS! – Cheers! / Mi salute

EXCUSE ME – Scuse mi / Mi a beg yuh

GETTING AROUND

WHERE IS THE BATHROOM? – Wha di bathroom deh?

WHAT TIME IS IT? – Wah time it?

HOW DO I GET TO...? – How mi fi get to...?

Where does this train/bus go?: Whe dis train/bus a go?

RESTAURANT – Ristorante (Same, just pronounced differently in Jamaican)

HOW MUCH DOES THIS COST? – How much dis cost?

TRAIN/METRO STATION – Train station / Metro station

COMMUNICATION

DO YOU SPEAK ENGLISH? – Yuh speak English?

I DO NOT UNDERSTAND – Mi nuh understand

I DON'T SPEAK ITALIAN – Mi nuh speak Italian

I DON'T KNOW – Mi nuh know

EMERGENCY

HELP! – Help mi!

CALL AN AMBULANCE! – Call ambulance fi mi!

I NEED A DOCTOR – Mi need a doctor

POLICE – Police

I'M LOST – Mi lost

IT'S AN EMERGENCY – A emergency dis

GLOSSARY

ACQUITTAL: A jury verdict that a criminal defendant is not guilty, or the finding of a judge that the evidence cannot support a conviction.

ADVERSARY PROCEEDING: A lawsuit arising from a controversy that begins with filing a complaint.

AFFIDAVIT: A written statement made under oath.

APPEAL: A request made after a trial court has decided against one party in which the losing party asks a higher court to review the decision for legal error.

ARRAIGNMENT: A proceeding in which a criminal defendant is brought to court, told of the charges, and asked to plead guilty or not guilty.

BAIL: The temporary release of a person from jail when awaiting trial, on condition that a sum of money be lodged or deposited to guarantee an appearance in court.

BARRISTER: A lawyer admitted to plead at the Bar and who may try cases in superior court.

BURDEN OF PROOF: The duty to prove disputed facts.

CAUSE OF ACTION: A legal claim in a civil action.

COMPLAINT: A written statement that begins a civil lawsuit in which the plaintiff details the claims.

CONTRACT: An agreement between two or more persons to do something or to not do something.

CONVICTION: A judgment of guilt against a person charged with a crime.

CUSTOMS DUTY: A tariff or tax imposed on goods when transported across international borders.

COURT LIAISON: A person that coordinates with attorneys to perform administrative duties, such as scheduling witnesses, sharing information with law enforcement, and overseeing the reporting of cases to foreign embassies when applicable.

DAMAGES: Money that a defendant pays to a plaintiff in a civil case if the plaintiff wins.

DEFENDANT: 1) The individual against whom a civil claim is filed; 2) The individual against whom a criminal charge is filed.

FELONY: A serious crime, punishable by more than one year in prison.

MAGISTRATE: A judicial officer of a district court, who conducts initial proceedings in criminal cases, decides criminal misdemeanor cases, conducts many pretrial civil and criminal matters on behalf of district judges, and decides civil cases with the consent of the parties.

MISDEMEANOR: An offense punishable by one year or less in jail.

PLAINTIFF: A person or business that files a formal complaint with the court.

PLEA: In a criminal case, the answer of "guilty", "not guilty", or "no contest" in response to a criminal charge.

SOLICITOR: A lawyer who advises clients, represents them in lower court, and prepares cases for barristers to try in higher courts.

SOVEREIGN IMMUNITY: A legal doctrine by which the sovereign or the state (i.e. government) cannot commit a legal wrong and thus, it is immune from criminal and civil liability and cannot be sued.

STATUTE: A written law passed by a legislative body.

STATUTE OF LIMITATIONS: A statute prescribing a period of limitation to bring certain types of legal actions. If the action is not brought within that time, the person or entity (in a criminal context) is permanently barred from suing in court.

SUBPOENA: A command, issued under court authority, for a witness to appear and to give testimony.

TESTIMONY: Evidence presented orally by witnesses.

VERDICT: The decision of a judge or jury in a case.

WARRANT: Court authorization to conduct a search or to make an arrest.

ACKNOWLEDGMENTS

This book series would never have seen the light of day without the able assistance of the following people:

Kathy Adams, my paralegal for over 22 years, who is the "Best" I've ever worked with during my entire legal career because of her amazing work ethic, organizational skills, and her ability to think outside of the box in unique and creative ways;

Ally Knez-Siddique, a professional writer, and one of my paralegals, whose eye for detail, according to her, is both a blessing and a curse;

Gino Ibanez, my former law clerk, whose exceptional research skills helped move this book series along in its early stages;

Rosa Diaz Graham, my legal assistant who helped with research and word processing at the very beginning of this project;

Shelia Martin, one of my former paralegals, worked diligently on this series of books, even after taking on another job. Her organizational skills are reflected throughout;

Mindy Scarlett, my marketing and publishing "Guru"! Her creativity and vision have no boundaries!

ABOUT THE AUTHOR

Michael L. Moore practices in Orlando, Florida, the city where he spent his formative years. He credits the trauma of having his brother murdered when he was only 10 years old, as the catalyst that drew him into the practice of law.

Moore attended Florida State University, where he was a member of the FSU debate team. Upon graduating, he was awarded a full scholarship to attend the University of Tennessee College of Law, where he was elected President of the Student Bar Association. He further honed his advocacy and public speaking skills by participating in 'moot court' competitions.

After clerking at the Tennessee Attorney General's office while in law school, Moore moved back to Orlando, Florida, to work at the State Attorney's Office as a prosecutor, and where he was fortunate enough to meet the young lady that would eventually become his wife. Moore moved on to working for private law firms, both local and national, and eventually established his own law firm in 1999. He continues to make Orlando his home base.

It was the murder of a close friend and client in Jamaica that caused Moore to realize that books on laws in other countries were few and far between, and he was inspired to create Law of the Land Publishing. Moore launched Law of the Land Publishing to provide a series of guidebooks and a membership site for tourists and business travelers to stay up to date on the laws in each country they travel to, as well as having access to assistance if they run into legal issues.

"My vision is to educate people on what their legal rights are, and how they can access legal assistance, no matter where they have to travel to in the world," said Moore. "As Americans, we have a right to due process, but in some countries, you don't even have the right to access a square meal when incarcerated. My goal is to provide the information needed to stay out of trouble, as well as having access to assistance if trouble finds you."

www.ingramcontent.com/pod-product-compliance
Lightning Source LLC
Chambersburg PA
CBHW051139120626
46547CB00012B/870